Move Over Extroverts

How to Build a Successful Real Estate Career as an Introvert

Ashley Harwood

Finesse Literary Press Ltd.

Copyright © 2025 by Ashley Harwood.

All rights reserved.

No portion of this book may be reproduced in any form without written permission from the publisher or author, except as permitted by U.S. copyright law.

This publication is sold with the understanding that neither the author nor the publisher is engaged in rendering legal, investment, accounting or other professional services. While the publisher and author have used their best efforts in preparing this book, they make no representations or warranties with respect to the accuracy or completeness of the contents of this book and specifically disclaim any implied warranties of merchantability or fitness for a particular purpose. No warranty may be created or extended by sales representatives or written sales materials. The advice and strategies contained herein may not be suitable for your situation. You should consult with a professional when appropriate. Neither the publisher nor the author shall be liable for any loss of profit or any other commercial damages, including but not limited to special, incidental, consequential, personal, or other damages.

First edition 2025 published by Finesse Literary Press Ltd.

Contents

Foreword		1
Introduction		7
Part I		
Energy Management		
	1. Self-assessment	15
	2. Benefits of Being an Introvert - To the Agent and to the Client	23
	3. The Energy Battery	29
	4. Your Recharge List	31
	5. The Draining List	35
	6. Let's Talk About Loved Ones	39
	7. Dealing With Drainers	41
	8. How Physical and Mental Energy are Related	43
	9. The Joy Plan	45
	10. Managing Your Mental Load	49

11.	Saying NO	53
12.	Boundaries: Setting and Maintaining Them	57

Part II
Time Management

13.	Time-Blocking	65
14.	Color-Coding	69
15.	Use Your Recharging & Draining Lists Strategically	73
16.	Take Days Off	75
17.	Leverage (in Unexpected Places)	81
18.	The Irish Goodbye	85
19.	The Dreaded 20k+ Person Conference	87
20.	Solo Vacations	93

Part III
Lead Generation

21.	A Mindset Shift	99
22.	Choose Your Niche	101
23.	Use Your Joy List	105
24.	Hobbies, Charity, Groups, and Clubs	109
25.	Housewarming Parties	115
26.	Client Appreciation Events	119
27.	Cold Calling Expired Listings and FSBOs	125
28.	Direct Mail	127

29.	Open Houses (Part 1)	135
30.	Community Charity Drives	139
31.	Starting & Controlling the Conversation	143
32.	Navigating Networking Events	149
33.	Get Out of Your Comfort Zone (But Only for Ten Minutes)	153
34.	Relationship-Building	157
35.	Entrepreneurs' Guilt	159
36.	Social Media	161
37.	Create Your Lead Gen Plan	165

Part IV

Working With Clients (Without Burning Out)

38.	Working With Sellers	173
39.	Working With Buyers	179
40.	Open Houses (Part 2)	185
41.	Managing Communication	187
42.	Home Inspections and Closings	191
43.	Follow Up	193
44.	Working With Vendors	197
45.	Hiring Talent	201

Part V

Be a Proud Introvert Out in the World

46.	Should you tell people you're an introvert?	209
47.	Attracting Your Ideal Clients	213
48.	The Proud, Confident Introvert	215
49.	Talk it Out or Sit in Silence?	219
50.	No Excuses or Limitations	221
51.	Thriving in Real Estate Operations	225
52.	Morning Routine and Evening Wind Down	231
53.	The Fake Smile	235
54.	Find Peace and Become a Better Agent	237

Acknowledgements	239
References	241
Recommended Reading	245

Foreword

Written by Keith Krikorian

What does it mean to be an introvert in the real estate world? Well, as a self-proclaimed extrovert, I thought I knew. As you probably know, my girlfriend, Ashley Harwood, owns a coaching company called Move Over Extroverts. Through this company, she has taught, coached, and spoken to audiences of real estate agents that are introverts. She's helped them drastically change their businesses and lives and empowered them to be the best that they can be. Naturally, I thought I knew what I was talking about when it came to the subject. Turns out, I didn't. (Side note for Ashley, yes, I just admitted I was wrong... Savor it).

As I wrote about in my own book, *The Art of War for Real Estate Agents*, I had always defined an introvert as shy, somewhat reclusive, and avoiding people whenever possible. These are the people who I call and invite to a party or social event, and more often than not, they will politely decline. Not a big deal; I get it. Or at least I thought I did. It's been said that I am the loudmouth, attention-seeking extrovert, who from time to time will adopt several introverts and take them along with me on my adventures. I would allow them to be involved while I inserted myself into every conversation during any given situation. And it wasn't until one real estate conference that I learned the term introvert was a lot different than I had previously thought. Let me tell you all about it.

Several years ago, Ashley was booked to speak at the Triple Play real estate conference in Atlantic City, New Jersey. We drove down from Massachusetts, checked into our hotel room, and got ourselves settled in. Ashley was slated to speak about introverts in real estate twice the next day. The next morning, I was excited for her and proud of her, like I always am. She went up on stage in front of a room full of people and delivered her first speech of the day. I figured I would walk around the back of the room and take some pictures and videos of her delivering content for her social media platforms. But I didn't realize how much I was about to learn.

As Ashley always does, she spoke softly, calmly, and purposefully. Her lecture was soothing and comfortable to listen to. The crowd was completely enamored and in tune with everything she said. Everyone was taking notes and hanging on every word. At one point, some of her words started to catch my attention as well. I listened more intently as I fumbled around, trying to get the right angle to capture on video.

Ashley said calmly and coolly: "An extrovert replenishes their energy in a social situation or in a crowd with other people. An introvert replenishes their energy alone." I realized... damn... I had never thought of it that way. She continued to speak about protecting energy, protecting your calendar, lead generation, and more.. I definitely heard things for the first time. I took just as much out of Ashley's speech as the introverts in the crowd. I recognized my own inability to judge some of the social situations I was in.

She crushed it. People were overwhelmed with gratitude to hear someone detail what they were going through. After her speech, crowds of people came up to introduce themselves and further discuss the topic. While I had just learned a lot myself, I was feeling excited and happy for her, and I was still taking it all in.

After everyone left, we went back to our hotel room. There were a few hours before she had to speak again, and while I was naturally congratulating her on a dynamite speech, I had thoughts I wanted to share. I thought of all the times I had gone on stage to speak in front of crowds. I am always super high energy and very passionate about everything I do, which is evident when I am on a stage or teaching a class. So I said to her: "Hon, that was amazing! I wonder, with a room full of introverts who might be a little nervous to speak in front of people, wouldn't they want to see you, an introvert, show them how they might be able to bring a certain level of energy to public speaking?" She said, "No, they just sat through a couple days of speakers that were loud, high energy presenters, all trying to rally the crowd. What I gave them was a calm, quiet space for them to learn in, just the way I would want it." Again, what I thought I knew might not have been correct.

I thought of all of the times I would go on a couple of listing appointments, run back to my office and teach a class, then shoot down the road and host/moderate a panel of top real estate agents in front of one hundred spectators. Naturally, that was followed by a social/networking hour in which I was shaking hands with everybody in the room, needing to be the center of attention. The event would end, and I would look at the remaining twenty people in the room and say: "Let's go to the cigar bar! Casino? Sure! Let's go!" And then I would look over at Ashley, who was more than willing to go, yet she looked like she would give anything in the world to go home, sit on our couch with a glass of wine and our cat nestled in her lap, watch several episodes of *Friends*, and relax for the rest of the night.

I was also barraged with memories of situations with friends of mine who fit into the stereotypical "introvert" persona. I remembered how I would be passionately talking their ears off about anything from empire building to real estate transactions to the New England Patriots game from the day before. More than once, a good friend of mine would look at me and say: "Darling, you're killing me with your energy right now." And I recognized that while I thought I was bringing a positive, energetic conversation to the table, I was really draining their batteries down, when what they needed was just to get away for a little bit and chill out. So many situations were pouring through my mind, times that I may have misread social interactions.

When we returned to our hotel room, Ashley said, "I think I'm going to take a quick nap."

I replied, "But... but... there's a casino right there. There is a cigar bar there," I continued, pointing out the window to the buildings adjacent to the hotel.

She said, "You should go. Have fun!"

In typical "Keith fashion," I lit a cigar, walked to the casino, and made a dozen new friends. I handed out business cards and received some as well. I picked up a referral and had a great time. I looked at my watch, and realized I should head back over to the hotel. As I walked into our room, there was Ashley, sitting upright in bed with her laptop open, clicking away at the keys. "Did you have a good nap?" I asked.

"I did," she replied.

"What are you doing now?" I asked.

"Booking a couple other speaking gigs and putting in applications to some conferences that want me to speak."

It all made sense. She had delivered a dynamite presentation in front of a crowded room and needed to recharge. She took her nap, booked more speaking gigs, and was ready to return to the conference and do it all over again. However, I kept on the throttle, and my energy was still at a high level, ready to cheer her on. To the introverts reading this, forgive my ignorance when I say that maybe Ashley is on to something.

Why am I sharing all of this? Well, I've learned that when I'm dealing with people on the introverted side, I need to be careful not to suck the life out of their social batteries. What feels like a fun environment to me might be a little draining for others, and I need to act accordingly and remember how my energy might affect other people. I've also learned how to better teach and coach my fellow real estate agents while being more mindful of what they are feeling.

What you are about to learn in the pages that follow will help you manage your own energy, generate leads in ways that are comfortable and more effective for you and your personality, manage a calendar that is mindful of who you are, help you be the best version of yourself that you can be, and so much more. While I do not put a ton of stock into labeling certain character traits, I've learned that I am more of an ambivert. Who knew? I hope you leave your journey through the following book with the same enlightenment and empowerment that so many others have. I'm grateful for all that I've learned from Ashley and wish you luck in your pursuit of your own version of quiet success.

Introduction

I have a terrible memory. The months and years bleed into one another. So I cannot tell you what season of the year it was or whether it was 2015 or 2016 when I first discovered that I am an introvert. But I do vividly recall driving my car, listening to a particular audiobook, and feeling overwhelmed by several unexpected emotions: the excitement of an epiphany, followed closely by the calm of relief.

I had heard the term "introvert" before, but I never gave it much thought. I certainly did not understand what it meant. If asked, I would have given the most common response: "Introverts are shy, quiet, and don't like people." I was highly social at this point in my real estate career, and I was also burning myself out all the time without realizing it. Reading that book helped me understand myself and make important changes to how I structured my real estate business, which led to my becoming a top-producing agent in the Boston, Massachusetts area.

You may be wondering if it's even possible for an introvert to build a successful career as a real estate agent. From the outside, these do not seem to naturally go together. I'm on a mission to prove the exact opposite is true: Introverts actually make incredible real estate agents, and there are many success stories out there. I'll share more details from my own journey in the next section, and you'll hear from some of the other top agents in the country to support this thesis throughout the book.

This is not a purely motivational book, although I hope you'll feel motivated, energized, and empowered after reading it. This book is intended to be a hands-on guide with action steps you can start implementing immediately. My goal is to give you your own sense of relief. I plan to fill in one of the significant gaps in the real estate training and leadership world: No one's talking about introversion in real estate—until now. Here is what's to come:

In Part I, you'll learn how to intentionally manage your energy to avoid burning out. If you're already deep into burnout right now, skip ahead to chapter 3, where you'll learn how to recharge your batteries. By the end of Part 1, you'll be well-equipped to conserve your energy as a precious resource and use it wisely as a tool in your business.

Part II is about managing your time. Once you know how to best spend your energy, the next step is how that translates into your calendar. We will also cover how to take days off as a solo real estate agent without a team, which is one of the most commonly requested topics from the agents I've coached and trained over the years.

Part III addresses most real estate agents' biggest challenge: how to find more clients. It's the lead generation section, where we'll dive into several different strategies for attracting new business, all of which are based around conserving your energy and utilizing your time in the best way possible. I'll teach you how to choose lead gen strategies that align with you as an individual (and an introvert) and show you how that alignment is critical to generating even better results. As a thank you for buying this book, you'll have access to my collection of free bonuses, available at www.MoveOverExtroverts.com/Bonus. Included in the bonuses is a list of over eighty additional lead generation strategies.

Part IV is about working through the real estate transaction process, from contract to close, as an introvert. What's the best way to handle running open houses or showing ten homes in one day without completely burning yourself out? We'll talk about boundaries, expectation setting, and treating your real estate business like a legitimate business rather than a time-sucking and expensive hobby.

Part V is where it all ties together. We'll discuss how to thrive as a proud introvert out in the world—dealing with other people in the best way possible while respecting your own needs. This is an important section that transcends real estate; the lessons we talk about in this section apply to all areas of life.

My goal is to give you all the tools and resources you need to be your best self as a human, business owner, and real estate agent, without feeling like you need to change who you are or squeeze yourself into an "extroverted box" to be successful. You don't. You have everything you need already within you; this book will simply help you identify those characteristics, draw them out, and use them to your advantage unapologetically. You will be more confident, empowered, and excited to go out into the world as the powerful introvert you are. Let's begin with energy management, which is at the core of everything we do.

Part I

Energy Management

Finesse Literary Press Ltd.

Part I

"Being a successful introvert entrepreneur requires that we be intentional about our energy. We have to create processes and approaches that support our personality and style. When it comes to marketing and sales, one size does not fit all."

Beth Buelow, The Introvert Entrepreneur

One

Self-assessment

Before we get into how to find more clients or how to restructure the calendar to take more time off, we must first deeply understand ourselves and how our energy operates. This is unique to every individual. By the end of this chapter, you'll be able to identify how your own personal energy ebbs and flows. That knowledge is the foundation we will build on throughout the rest of the book. You'll be able to use this knowledge to conserve your energy when needed and flourish in the people-centric business of real estate.

Managing energy is a crucial component of any entrepreneur's success. It's important to know where to spend your energy in order to maximize your return. You have likely heard of return on investment (ROI), and maybe you've even heard of return on energy (ROE). ROE is a type of ROI that is focused on where you spend your energy versus where you spend your money. What's the highest and best use of your energy in any given moment? Where will your input bring you the best output?

For example, having coffee with a friend who consistently refers clients to you is likely a better investment of energy than attending the office holiday party. For me, a one-on-one coffee date requires less energy than making small talk in a loud restaurant with people I see all the time, and it's much more likely to result in additional business. That's a much better use of energy. In order to determine your highest and best ROE, you'll need to start with understanding how your individual energy works.

As introverts, we recharge our energy batteries differently than extroverts. If you haven't yet read Susan Cain's best-selling book *Quiet*, add it to your Amazon cart right now. Reading Cain's ground-breaking book on introversion completely changed my understanding of how my brain and nervous system work, leading me to make significant changes in my business and life (yes, this is the audiobook I talked about in the introduction). I reference *Quiet* several times throughout this book, starting with one of the best summaries I've ever read about introversion:

> "Many psychologists would agree that introverts and extroverts work differently. Extroverts tend to tackle assignments quickly. They make fast (sometimes rash) decisions, and are comfortable multitasking and risk-taking...Introverts often work more slowly and deliberately...Introverts may have strong social skills and enjoy parties and business meetings, but after a while wish they were home in their pajamas...They listen more than they talk, think before they speak,

> and often feel as if they express themselves better in writing than in conversation."
>
> — Cain, Quiet

If you're like me, this resonates with you in a powerful way. And when we think about how to recharge our energy batteries, alone time is the key. I certainly need my alone time, and I feel completely drained if too much time passes without it or expend too much energy in a short burst.

Of course, everyone is different, and each of us is a beautiful blend of introversion and extroversion. Think of it like a spectrum. At each end are extreme introverts and extreme extroverts. You can probably think of examples of both from your own network of friends, family, and clients. Most of us fall somewhere between the extremes.

When I first launched Move Over Extroverts, my coaching company for introverts, most of my friends and colleagues were surprised. They asked: "Are you really an introvert? How is that possible? You're so social!" And my response was and still is: "Yes, and being so social is incredibly draining. So I'll be leaving soon to take a nap." Many of us are very social, not always because we enjoy it, but because being a real estate agent somewhat necessitates it. We are in a people business. But don't let that scare you. My mission is to empower you, my fellow introvert working in real estate, and show you how to be successful without changing who you are or pretending to be someone you are not.

Let's learn more about who you are. I developed a completely anecdotal and non-scientific quiz to help you identify where on the introvert/extrovert spectrum you fall. Thousands of real estate agents have taken this quiz and about ten percent are truly surprised by the results. The reason? Many of us are masquerading as extroverts! I was one of them. Through no fault of our own, we act like extroverts because it's the default personality setting in the world of real estate. If you don't know better, you'll fall into the trap. And the result, if you're like me, will be detrimental to your mindset, your health, and your business.

Take a moment and take the quiz for yourself:

1. You're planning a night out. Which sounds more fun?

    a. Going out with a group of friends

    b. Dinner with your best friend, just the two of you

2. As a student, would you rather...

    a. Listen to an interesting lecture

    b. Participate in a lively discussion

3. After attending a large networking event, do you usually feel...

    a. Tired and drained, even if you had a good time

    b. Energized and excited for the next one

4. In general, which statement is most true for you?

    a. I love multi-tasking and am good at it.

    b. I prefer working on one thing at a time, staying focused.

5. You and a friend have a disagreement. How would you most likely react?

   a. I tell them how I feel and don't hold back my thoughts.

   b. I remain quiet in the moment and bring it up after giving myself time to process and develop a plan for what to say.

6. When you sit down to cold call a list of expired listings, is your gut instinct to...

   a. Research each lead, review your notes, and think through what they might say.

   b. Dial as quickly as possible and get through the list.

7. Your last appointment or call of the day reschedules on you. What's your reaction?

   a. I'm frustrated I won't make the sale today and get back to work to make another appointment.

   b. I'm relieved and thankful to have an extra hour or two to myself.

8. Have you ever questioned whether you have the "right personality" for this career?

   a. Yes

   b. No

9. If you attend an event where you only know a few people, are

you more likely to...

a. Approach a stranger, introduce yourself, and make a new contact.

b. Find someone you know and talk to them first.

10. Does the thought of talking to 100 people every week make you feel

a. Excited about all the new business it will bring

b. Terrified about having to talk to so many people

The introvert answers are: 1-B, 2-A, 3-A, 4-B, 5-B, 6-A, 7-B, 8-A, 9-B, 10-B

How did you do? If you scored 1-4, you are likely more extroverted. If you're right around a 5, you probably are an ambivert. And if you scored 6-10, you fall more on the introverted side of the spectrum. Remember—there are no right or wrong answers, only greater self-awareness. Hopefully, you have a bit more clarity about your own energetic patterns and can start to build your awareness going forward.

None of this is easy. Knowing yourself on a deep level and mastering energy management takes time, effort, and consistency. Paying attention to how your energy works is a new habit that most of us need to build. We aren't taught this in school. We aren't even taught it in most real estate classes (unless you've taken my classes, of course). Give yourself grace. Be patient with yourself. Working as a real estate agent requires a lot of interaction with other people, and there's no getting around that fact. The key for us is to embrace it and purposefully use our natural strengths as introverts to better serve our clients.

Two

Benefits of Being an Introvert - To the Agent and to the Client

Society holds a grave misconception about us introverts. People think we aren't well-suited to socially-taxing industries like real estate, but they are wrong. Plain and simple. Some of the top agents and leaders in the real estate industry are actually introverts: Gary Keller, Ryan Serhant, and Ben Kinney to name a few. In this chapter, we'll cover the benefits of being an introvert and how you can use your unique introvert strengths to be an incredible real estate agent.

What makes a great real estate agent? Grab your pen and paper and make a quick list. You probably included qualities such as: attentive listener, asks a lot of questions, builds deep relationships, and pays attention to detail.

If you've found yourself on the introverted side of the scale, you're in luck. Most qualities that make a fantastic real estate agent also come naturally to most introverts. Of course, there are exceptions to every general statement (such as the statements I'll be making in this section), yet introverts are generally gifted real estate agents because of how we are wired. When meeting new people, we prefer cutting out the small talk and getting to the core of who the other person is quickly. This helps us build strong relationships efficiently and easily. Then it's a matter of keeping in touch and staying top of mind with these new connections.

When I began building my real estate business in 2013, I had to build a sphere of influence, a social network, from scratch. I had grown up in Michigan and moved to Massachusetts two years prior to starting my real estate career. During those two years, I'd worked in customer service at the luxury department store Neiman Marcus, and I had met a handful of neighbors who lived on the street I had recently moved to. I had no family nearby; I had no high school or college friends who lived in the state to be potential clients or referral sources.

Being an introvert, my energy was sucked dry every day at Neiman's, talking to customers with a smile plastered on my face, helping our sales associates manage complicated returns, and putting out customer-centric fires such as, "The shoes I paid $1,200 for last week are now on sale for $800. Could I have a credit for the difference?" (These were high-level, significant life or death issues here!) It was tedious work and involved being "on" for eight hours per day.

However, it gave me an incredible customer service background to bring to real estate.

But I was in the unfortunate position, as you might be now, of needing to build a sphere from nothing—a daunting task. My database consisted of about fifty people, and I knew that was not enough to earn the income I desired or build the real estate empire I envisioned for my career. I had to find more people. So I started researching networking groups in the area. I attended every networking event I could find—chamber of commerce breakfast meetings, women's luncheons, after hours events, speed networking, referral groups, young professionals events, even a variety of Meetups. At every event, there were between twenty and five hundred people. It was overwhelming, especially in the beginning before I knew how to work a room my own way (don't worry—we have an entire chapter on how to network later in the book). At this point in my life, I had no idea what an introvert was, let alone that I was one, so my energy management was non-existent, and I was constantly in a state of energetic deficit.

Whenever I walked into a networking event when I knew no one, I felt extremely nervous. I beelined for the bar, bought either a glass of wine or a Diet Coke (for the purpose of having something in my hand), and made my way to one of the corners of the room. Eventually, I'd have a few conversations with people who approached me, and we would exchange business cards. Those conversations were generally very surface-level and painful to get through. Small talk and introverts don't mesh well. Have you ever had the most painful exchange in the history of the English language? You know the one: "Hi, how are you?" "Great! How are you?" "Good!" "That's good!" "Yeah!" then silence. Can you hear my eyes roll?

The purpose of attending the large events was to meet new people and start building relationships. The magic happened in the follow-up.

Each new person I met—as long as we clicked and I desired to get to know them —received a handwritten note from me in the mail. Just a simple "nice to meet you" note. And people loved them. Such a small gesture made a massive impact. I've actually received referrals because I sent a handwritten note, and it was so memorable. With a simple note in the mail, relationships deepen. If you aren't already using this technique, handwritten notes can be your new secret weapon, as it's extremely memorable, impactful, and doesn't require any social energetic output. You can even write them while at home with your cat watching *Love is Blind*.

People started thanking me for the cards at networking events. They knew who I was! Bingo. That's the key. Strategic, powerful, and efficient relationship building. Relationship-building is one of our introvert superpowers, and it's a key ingredient to being a successful real estate agent. Use it to your advantage, and know that you are well-equipped to build an incredible business and help a lot of people.

Your introvert superpowers are also beneficial to your clients. Let's talk about listening. There are entire courses and books dedicated to teaching salespeople how to listen. Not knowing you personally, I'd say you're probably a better listener than many of the other agents in your office, better than the loud, outgoing person who's always bragging about their latest deals, drives a flashy car, and is more concerned with their total GCI than their clients' experience. I'm making assumptions and grossly generalizing here, but you understand my point.

MOVE OVER EXTROVERTS

Actively listening, asking questions, going three deep in your questions, taking good notes, and truly desiring to understand the clients' needs are the pillars of a great real estate agent, a great salesperson in any industry. For most introverts, these skills come naturally. Embrace them. Use them. Build your confidence knowing that you possess the keys to success already. There are a lot of people who think introverts can't be great real estate agents, and they are wrong. You were born to help people, so I encourage you to go find more people to help.

Three

The Energy Battery

My favorite analogy for energy management is the cell phone battery. By the end of this chapter, you'll have a new tool for tracking your energy and identifying how much "battery power" you have at any given moment. Use this tool to avoid burning out and make strategic decisions about where to spend your energy.

You plug your phone in at night, and the battery recharges fully. As soon as you unplug it from the wall, the battery starts to drain. It's slow, but it is draining, simply by not being actively charging. When you open it and start using apps, it drains faster. Certain apps drain it faster than others. Watching YouTube videos uses more battery power than sending a simple text. A regular phone call uses less power than a Facetime call.

You go through your day, calling, texting, scrolling on social media, checking email, and at some point, if you don't plug your phone into a charger, you'll see a scary red warning pop up that says "low battery." On most phones, this happens when the battery is at twenty percent of its charge. What's your low battery warning sign? We will cover this in more detail in a future chapter, but I'd encourage you to start thinking about it now.

If you still don't plug it in, the phone will eventually die. The equivalent consequence for us humans ranges anywhere from burning out and needing a few days off to serious physical problems, even ending up in the hospital. Building your own awareness about your energy and focusing on your energy management skills is vital. Do not take this part for granted.

Now, let's say you need to charge your phone quickly. A regular charge only goes so fast, but there are certain things you can do to help it go faster, such as turning it on airplane mode and closing all your apps. Everyone's energy operates the same way. When you think about your own energy, consider what things recharge it (rather than drain it) and what charges you the fastest and most efficiently. What's your equivalent to "airplane mode?"

Awareness is the first step; putting it into practice is a whole other habit to build. And sometimes you'll still go too hard and drain your battery. This happened to me this month. I started off this year with an abundance of energy and excitement. We had several new listings come on the market and all received multiple offers. I was working to find new leads everyday and saying yes to everything. After three weeks of this pace, I got sick. It was just a cold and only lasted a few days, but I could pinpoint exactly why my body had shut down: I hadn't recharged my mental or physical batteries enough. So build the habits of recharging your energy, and know it's okay to slip up sometimes. No one is perfect!

Four

Your Recharge List

Now that you know how critical it is to be aware of your energy to manage it, let's get into the more practical ways to track the activities that recharge your individual energy. This will be different for each of us.

How can you more easily discover how your own energy recharges? I'm sure some examples came to mind as you were reading the previous section. Write them down and keep a running list to add to as you think of more things. Your list of rechargers can include activities, people, and even places. There's no limit to what you can include; the goal is to have as many options for recharging as possible. This list is solely for you, so do your best not to judge anything that's on (or not on) the list. We'll refer to this as your Recharge List.

To help you create your Recharge List, here's an easy exercise: Print out a copy of your last four week's calendar (or make copies if you use a paper calendar). Go through each day and write a plus mark next to all the activities that made you feel replenished and a minus sign next to everything that drained your energy. Some people use two different colored highlighters for this exercise—do whatever works for you. Then study the data. You'll start to see patterns. If you need more data points, go back two or three months or more. Get as much information you need to identify your patterns.

Now, use those patterns to fill out your Recharge List. The longer the list, the better. Ideally, your list will have a combination of free and paid activities and a variety of time commitments, such as thirty seconds to several days and everything in between. The reason for including so much variety is to allow you to pull items from the list and fit them strategically into your calendar as you build out your week. We'll talk more about this in the Time Management section. Keep this list somewhere easily accessible to you.

To give you some ideas, my personal Recharge List includes walking outdoors, taking a nap, reading fiction, attending a hot yoga class, watching TV, shopping, cooking, grocery shopping (but only if it's first thing in the morning and the store is empty), and spending time with Keith and our crazy orange cat, Marty.

Meet mega agent Chelsea Anderson, a good friend of mine who runs the highly successful Andersen Signature Team out of Tempe, Arizona. She generously shared her wisdom and experience as a top agent running a team as an introvert. You will hear from her several times throughout the book. (Please keep her team in mind for referrals in Arizona!)

> "I have systems built into my day to allow me to recharge. If days are especially taxing, I go sit by the river for ten minutes and just touch the rocks with my hands and let my feet soak in the water. It regrounds

me enough to head home to deal with my children before bed."

Chelsea Anderson

So start your list now and never stop adding to it. This is a living, breathing list that will serve you for the rest of your life, if you choose to use it. Once a year, go through and remove anything that's no longer recharging you the way it should. Things change as we go through different seasons of life, and it's okay to add, change, and delete items from your list. For a downloadable pdf Recharge List, visit the bonus section available at www.MoveOverExtroverts.com/Bonus.

Five
The Draining List

Recharging activities are a helpful tool in managing your energy. Knowing when and how to bring your energy level back up will set you up for success, ensure you're bringing your highest energy to the most important parts of your day, and help you avoid burning out. Equally critical is building your awareness of everything/everyone that drains your energy. As you strive for balanced energy throughout your day-to-day life, this information is crucial.

So how do you know what drains you? Again, you probably have examples coming to mind. Add those to the top of your Draining List. For more activities, people, or places to include on your list, go back to the data you collected from studying your calendar and make your list of things that drained you.

My own Draining List includes having tough conversations (example: telling a buyer their offer didn't get accepted), too much noise, crowds, 1:1 meetings, conferences, and phone calls.

An important note on the Draining List: You can enjoy something, and it can also be on the draining list. For me, conferences are a perfect example. I love attending conferences. I love speaking at conferences. I love networking at conferences. I love meeting people in person at conferences, people who I've only connected with on social media or via Zoom. And they are incredibly draining. I will skip educational sessions, dinners out, and wild nights on the town to sustain my energy. I need more naps during conferences than at any other time.

I know you heard this story already, and that was Keith's perspective. Here's mine: The first time I spoke at a tri-state regional conference and had two sessions in one day, I went straight up to my room and took a nap after the first session. Keith thought I was crazy (he's very much an extrovert, as you know). We were in Atlantic City. He was shocked I didn't want to go explore the casino and gamble with strangers. I told him I would love to explore and gamble, but I needed some down time to recharge my batteries before teaching my next session. Thankfully, I was self-aware enough to recognize what I needed and articulate it, defend it, and make it happen. I buried myself under the covers, closed the drapes, and took a nice hour-long nap. I woke up refreshed. I taught my next session and brought my best energy to the attendees in the room. For the record, we did end up staying out late that night, but I waited until I was finished with my important commitments.

I recently heard about a concept called the "social hangover," a phenomenon that often occurs for us introverts after extended social engagement. I definitely have experienced that. If you ever feel this way, it's a sign the activity needs to live on your Draining List. Again, do not judge your list!

Realizing you can enjoy something and still be drained by it is key because often we think we need to eliminate all draining things from our lives, but that's not always the case. It's not even usually the case. More often than not, a simple rearranging of the schedule is the solution. The awareness around what drains you and what energizes you is key, so you can manage your energy around it and still do all the things you enjoy.

Six

Let's Talk About Loved Ones

Loved ones get their own chapter, as they're often the exceptions to all the norms I'm talking about in this book. Some family members are the worst energy drainers (looking at everyone who has kids, am I right?). And some loved ones are not energy sucks at all. For example, I spend most of my free time with Keith. I need time alone from everyone in the world except him because he's my person. Side note: If you're looking for the right romantic partner for you, find a person who doesn't drain you while spending lots of time together. It's rare and magical when you find it.

Several years ago, I taught a full-day class for a real estate brokerage in the Northeast. One of the agents in the class was struggling with his conversion rates on his listing appointments. We talked through his routine leading up to the appointment to try to establish his mindset and energy going into those high-stakes meetings. After a series of questions, we discovered he had unintentionally built the habit of calling his mother on the drives over to meet with the sellers. It seemed like an excellent use of time. He's in the car anyway—might as well check "call mom" off the to-do list. As it turned out, those conversations were affecting his energy in a detrimental way. He was sabotaging every listing appointment he went on without even realizing it. It was a major "aha" moment for him.

He made the decision during that class to call her after the appointment, not before. This tiny change helped him improve his conversion rate, take more listings, and earn more money—all because he shifted the timing of a phone call. This is the power of understanding where your energy drains are and making strategic decisions about timing. We will delve deeper into this concept in the Time Management section.

Now, this is not to say you should excommunicate anyone who drains your energy. Not at all. But being aware of who drains and who recharges you can make a massive difference in your life and your business. It can feel uncomfortable to list people on your Draining List. I know. But I give you permission and encouragement to include people on your lists. Remember: These lists are for your eyes only. It's simple data collection, nothing more. Release any guilt you may feel. Acknowledging that an individual drains your energy does not mean you care about or love the person any less. It will help you be more strategic in your communication and interactions with them. Call your mom—after the appointment.

Seven

Dealing With Drainers

Talking about the Draining List isn't the most uplifting topic, but it's vital to understand who and what your drainers are and decide how to handle each one. This exercise will help you streamline your energy decisions to be more efficient, productive, and experience more ease. Better results with less stress—that's the goal!

Review your list of energy drainers. For each item on the list, you have four options:

1. Eliminate it from your life entirely.

2. Delegate it—hire leverage or ask someone else to do it.

3. Reschedule it.

4. Do nothing and increase your awareness.

Here are a few specific examples: If your children drain you (and how could they not, seriously?), you're not going to eliminate them, delegate them, or reschedule them. But you can and should increase your awareness around how they affect your energy. And that's powerful in itself.

If grocery shopping in a crowded store drains you, either option two or three would be your best bet. You can't eliminate it, but you can hire someone else to do it for you (grocery delivery services used to be an elite thing, but now they're very common and inexpensive) or reschedule it and go when it's less crowded. I do this; I love grocery shopping, but it's only enjoyable when I have the place to myself. Fighting crowds and standing in lines ruins the fun for me.

If posting on social media drains you, you can always hire someone or eliminate it and replace it with a different lead generation strategy. We'll cover this in more detail in the lead gen section.

Eight

How Physical and Mental Energy are Related

Have you ever been accused of being hangry? When my blood sugar is low, and I haven't taken in enough calories for the day, it affects my mood. The slang term for this is "hangry," a combination of "hungry" and "angry." This is a perfect example of how physical and mental energy are connected. I'm not a doctor, nutritionist, or scientist, so I'll be talking in general terms, using purely anecdotal evidence from my own experience. Please don't sue me. Always consult with your medical professional.

My most compelling trigger for knowing when I'm low on mental energy is when I'm feeling irritable. I don't think clearly. My communication gets short, snippy. I lose my patience more easily. It's more difficult for me to problem solve effectively because my annoyance at small things clouds my judgment. This is when I know I need to recharge my energy.

All of these triggers are exacerbated when my physical energy is low from lack of sleep, lack of calories, empty calories from poor (yet delicious) food choices, dehydration, and not enough exercise. If I skip hot yoga for several weeks, I feel it, and it affects my mental energy.

Think about times when your physical energy has affected your mental energy. If you're able to, take a break right now and journal some of these instances. Bringing awareness to this connection is very helpful, even if it takes time to understand how they're connected within yourself.

Nine
The Joy Plan

What if we could guarantee joy in our lives? What if we could bake it right into the schedule to ensure it happens? What's the point of working so hard and building an incredibly successful business if we aren't taking time to do the things that bring us joy? We can and ought to prioritize joy. This will make each of us happier, healthier, and yes, more productive.

There's also something psychologically powerful about having something to look forward to. It pulls us through the mundane. It helps us stay motivated when we are feeling discouraged or hit a roadblock. I've known this to be true for years, yet only recently have I created a system for ensuring I'll always have something joyful to look forward to.

You've likely heard of a Growth Plan. Maybe you've even created a growth plan before. And growth plans are valuable business tools; they help you continue to learn and improve your skills as a business owner and leader. I always advise having a growth plan with at least one self-improvement activity, book, or conference scheduled each month during the year.

Now let's take this concept and apply it to joy. Create a Joy Plan! For your Joy Plan, the structure is the same as a growth plan, yet the intention is completely different. The key here is joy, however you define it. It could be happiness, contentment, euphoria, relaxation, thrill, rest, or all of the above. The Joy Plan is not about personal development, not learning, not leadership, not sales. Purely joy.

This is a new concept for many of us. In the business world, and especially in the real estate industry, there's not much focus on joy. Over the past few years, I've seen more conversations around mental health, work/life balance, avoiding burnout (okay, I may have written the class on that one), and putting family first. All of those are vital to your success in real estate and your success as a human. Joy has been a missing piece of the conversation until now.

Almost all of the real estate agents I talk to are so laser-focused on building their businesses that they don't create space for joy, for fun. I advocate not only creating space for it but prioritizing it.

Practically, this is what it looks like: Make a list of things you already enjoy or know would bring you joy. Aim to make this list as long and robust as possible. Include things you've always dreamed of doing in addition to activities you currently do. This is even a perfect opportunity to integrate your bucket list. Then schedule at least one item from your list every month. Do not skip a month! Go ahead and schedule more if you can, but one per month is a solid, realistic start for most people.

Unlike the energy recharge list, this list should primarily consist of things that need to be booked in advance because those are more challenging to cancel, and the likelihood of you following through with your plans increases. Avoid the potential self-sabotage.

Once you plan and execute your joy list, you'll feel more peaceful and energized. Having joyful things to look forward to throughout the year will bring a different energy to your day-to-day life. Your family, friends, and colleagues will likely notice the difference. When they ask you about it, please share this strategy with them. Spread the word, and the world will become a more peaceful, joyful place.

You'll find a downloadable pdf template in the bonus section to help you create your own Joy Plan.

Ten

Managing Your Mental Load

Mental load is a relatively new concept, at least for me. I learned about it while reading a novel called *The Wife App* by Carolyn Mackler. In the book, a group of women develop a mobile app that provides help to overworked mothers and their ever-growing lists of household and family responsibilities. A major part of the stress these characters felt came from carrying the mental load for their families.

UCLA Health defines mental load as "the 'thinking' work you do daily," such as remembering which groceries to buy, when to schedule the kids' orthodontic appointments, what day to pick up the dry cleaning, which houses your buyer wants to see this week, when the photographer is scheduled for your newest listing, and when the closing date was moved to (did I remember to tell the client about the changed date?). I could write another entire book simply listing mental load items, but I doubt that would be a fun or informative read for anyone.

The key to managing your mental load is mental leverage. I'd been using mental leverage for years without knowing what it was or having a name for it. Mental leverage can take many forms. My favorites are:

- Setting phone reminders that pop up at a specific time

- Scheduling emails and social media posts ahead of time

- Hiring a transaction coordinator to manage the contract to close process

- Keeping an ongoing grocery list in the notes app on my phone

- Journaling

- Having one dedicated place to write notes throughout the day

These last two save me a significant amount of mental energy because once I write something down, I no longer need to actively store it in my mind. I've freed up mental space.

Let's talk about journaling a bit more. If I could only recommend one strategy for managing your mental load, it would be journaling. Writing things down helps me not only remove them from my brain and make space in my mind, but it also helps me organize my thoughts and work through anything that's causing me stress. My journal is where I make lists, rant, dream, set goals, and problem solve. Some of my very best ideas have come from the act of journaling.

MOVE OVER EXTROVERTS

Now, the mechanics of how you journal can be tailored to your preferences. Some people prefer an oral journal—talking into your voice memo app or another voice recording device. Some people like to type. I am old fashioned and prefer paper journals and felt tip pens. Something about the physical action of moving the pen on the paper is soothing, almost therapeutic. And I always feel better after getting my thoughts down on paper, even when I go into a journal session with nothing specific in mind. If you've never tried it, give it a try and see if you like it.

Eleven

Saying NO

Think about the last time you said yes and immediately regretted it. It happens to everyone who hasn't mastered the art of saying no. This chapter will teach you how to say no kindly and without apology. You will be able to get so much of your time back after mastering the art of saying no.

Saying no is a skill and a habit to build. It's also difficult. Most of us struggle with saying no, as we're people-pleasers. Real estate agents especially are conditioned to always say yes. "I'm available 24/7!" or "Of course we can go see that property, even though it's outside your budget!" We bend over backward for our clients (and leads who are not even clients yet), sometimes to the detriment of the other person. Showing a property priced too far outside of a client's budget is harmful to the client and a huge waste of your time. We answer our phones at midnight and train our clients to expect immediate responses at all hours.

We do this out of fear. We fear our clients will fire us, our leads will hire someone else, and we won't be able to pay our bills. People-pleasing stems from a lack of confidence and a lack of business. I know it's not popular to say, but it's the truth. When we have enough leads to feed the business, it's much easier to say no. When we are confident in ourselves, it's much easier to say no (check out the book *The Full Fee Agent* by Chris Voss and Steve Shull for more on this particular topic).

I say this with love. We have to stop people-pleasing. We have to learn to say no for our own sake, our families' sake, and our clients' sake.

Think about the things you've said yes to in the past month. Keep in mind that when you say yes to one thing, you say no to something else. What have you said yes to? What do those yeses automatically mean you're saying no to? Make a list in your journal.

Taking on a leadership role in your networking group means less time for other activities. Maybe that's a worthwhile investment of time and energy. Maybe it's not. Think about your yeses as investments. Everything you say yes to requires an investment of time, energy, money, or a combination of these. In determining whether to say yes or no, ask yourself one simple question: Will the investment be worth it? Keep in mind that at first, you may not know for sure. There are calculated risks you'll take, and you'll adjust course as necessary. But by approaching every decision through this lens, it will help you say yes to better investments and protect your resources by saying no more often.

> "If you understand yourself to know your energy limits, you cannot afford to waste any energy on somebody else's priorities, especially if they do not align with your own. If you say yes, you have to be able to

> manage the pool of energy that the YES will take for the entire term of the commitment, whether that is sitting on the board of an organization, helping with a school project, volunteering, signing up for a marathon… you must understand the amount of energy it will take to finish."
>
> Chelsea Anderson

How do you say no without losing a client, disappointing someone, or feeling badly about it? Say it earnestly and with empathy. Be direct. Be clear. My favorite collection of words for saying no is, "I wish I could, but I don't have the bandwidth at the moment." Another good response is, "Unfortunately, I won't be available then, but one of my colleagues would be happy to take care of it for you." We'll talk more about taking time off and communication around time off in a future chapter.

Keep in mind that people are much more accustomed to hearing no than to saying no. So it may feel uncomfortable for you to say no, but the person you're saying no to has heard the word plenty of times in their lifetime and won't be angry with you for saying it one more time. They will understand. They may even respect you more. You are in charge of your decisions. You are the CEO of your life. And you decide where you spend your investments of time, energy, and money.

Twelve

Boundaries: Setting and Maintaining Them

This final chapter of the Energy Management section of the book is all about boundaries. Many of us struggle with establishing boundaries, maintaining them, or both. By the end of this chapter, you'll have the tools you need to set and hold your chosen boundaries in your real estate business and in your personal life.

Boundaries are the manifestation of taking care of yourself first: your time, your energy, your mental space. And setting expectations is how you communicate your boundaries to others. Protect your energy. Setting clear boundaries and maintaining them are the keys to protecting your energy.

The first step is to determine what your boundaries are for yourself and in your business. Let's talk through a few different types of boundaries, so you can begin thinking about each one in detail. As you read through each type, write down your initial gut reaction (that's your intuition telling you the answer; listen to it). Then go back and analyze each one to make sure your intended boundary fits within your overall personal and professional goals and matches your desired lifestyle.

- Time. How early in the morning and how late into the evening will you return phone calls, emails, or texts? Is there a hard stop for each style of communication, or is there one specific hour of the night when you'll shut everything down? What about emergencies? What constitutes an emergency?

- People. Perhaps there's a person in your life who is taking up too much time or energy, and a boundary needs to be set regarding how often you communicate. Perhaps there are people who should not be in your life at all. Or maybe there are people in your life who are wonderful, add value, and should remain in your life, but there's too much unnecessary drama. I've seen that one before, many times—if the overall theme of your conversations is negative without being constructive, there may be an opportunity to set a boundary and essentially "buy back" some of your precious energy.

- Mental energy. This one is much more about your own inner monologue, how you deal with stress, pressure, and problems that arise. While I've gotten much better about setting boundaries with myself around my mental energy, it's still a challenge.

MOVE OVER EXTROVERTS

Example - Avoid "the sky is falling" syndrome: My team and I were told that the scheduled appraisal on a house we were selling had been canceled. My gut reaction was, "Okay, that's probably good news. The mortgage lender has issued an appraisal waiver and we no longer need an appraisal on this property." One of my colleagues jumped straight to, "Oh no, the buyer is backing out of the deal!" Now, my reaction was the result of years of re-training my mind and setting firm boundaries with myself about how I chose to react. I guarantee I used up a lot less mental energy than my colleague that day. My assumption was correct, and the deal closed without any issues.

After you've set your boundaries, which takes a finite amount of time and effort, now you need to maintain them, something that will never end but does get easier with time and practice. Practice, practice, practice, then stumble, get back up, and keep practicing. There's no magic bullet or step-by-step guide to maintaining boundaries. You have to just start and keep trying.

In some cases, it makes sense to explicitly communicate a boundary. This could look like a tough conversation between friends or colleagues. I'd usually recommend leaving this option as a last resort. Most of the time, adjusting your behavior and reactions will nudge the situation in the right direction. If your boundary is to stop working each night at 8 p.m., it's up to you to resist the urge to answer a text after that time (barring true emergencies, of course). Over time, you'll teach people how to communicate with you. In this example, you could also set the expectation with new clients ahead of time, telling them what your working hours are. People respect transparency and will understand that no one can be available literally twenty-four hours a day. In Part IV of this book, we'll dive deeper into managing your communication with clients, so no one expects you to answer the phone in the middle of the night.

Take Action:

- Conduct an energy audit: Go through your calendar from the past week and put a + or - next to each activity.

- List everything/everyone that replenishes and drains your energy.

- Choose how to deal with the drainers. Journaling could be productive to help you work through how you're going to deal with each drainer.

- Create your Joy Plan to balance your energy and enjoy the life you're creating.

- Identify where you need to set and/or enforce more boundaries, then start building the habit of sticking to your boundaries.

Part II

Time Management

Finesse Literary Press Ltd.

"Extraordinarily successful people launch their year by taking time out to plan their time off. Why? They know they'll need it, and they know they'll be able to afford it...Resting is as important as working."
>
> Gary Keller and Jay Papasan, The ONE Thing

Thirteen
Time-Blocking

Now that you've learned how to identify your energy patterns and better manage your energy input and output, you can use that information to better manage your time. This section on time management will help you create the ideal calendar for you in your business and your life to maximize productivity, avoid burnout, and increase your joy! We will even cover how to take days off as a solo agent without a team. The first step: time-blocking.

On its most basic level, time-blocking is determining ahead of time how you'll spend your minutes and hours each day. On a practical level, it's putting blocks of time in your calendar to focus on specific tasks. The benefit of doing this is you're taking control of your days and making sure the highest priority tasks get done. Of course, unexpected things come up, so it's perfectly fine to rearrange your time blocks. Be careful not to eliminate your money-making time blocks! For us real estate agents, lead generation and follow-up are crucial activities that must be on the calendar every work day (notice I did not say everyday; we need rest days too). If you need to schedule a showing at the last minute, be sure to reschedule your lead gen or lead follow up time block if it interferes.

Here are the steps to setting up your time blocks in the most effective way:

1. Block off your personal time *first*: solo vacations, full days off, half days off, exercise, hobbies, journaling time, morning and evening routines, kitten cuddle time, and anything else you're committed to doing for yourself.

2. Block off your family time next: family vacations, birthday parties, weddings, reunions, holidays, date nights with your spouse, and other commitments for family.

3. Make a list of everything you want/need to do for your business in a given week.

4. Rearrange the list in order of priority/importance. For example, each work day should contain time blocks for finding new business, following up on existing leads, and servicing your current clients.

5. Add your blocks of time to the calendar, starting at the top of your list.

One crucial tip to keep in mind: Leave white space on your calendar. Better yet, create a separate time block called White Space. This is time you'll use to catch up on emails, return phone calls, and take care of all those little things that come up over the course of the day. The timing of your white space blocks is up to you, and each person has their own preferences. For me, a block first thing in the morning and another in the afternoon works well. That way, I can catch up on anything from the night before and really dive into my important tasks without wondering if something needs my immediate attention, and I have a second opportunity to catch up in the late afternoon before calling it a night.

White Space is different from Thinking Space. Thinking Space requires its own time block as well. This is pure quiet time where you are by yourself, usually in nature if the weather allows, and you have the space (no pun intended) to just think. The brain gets more creative when we aren't trying to force it. Some of my best thinking comes when I'm walking outdoors, alone, letting my mind wander as it processes everything it's been through lately.

Leave yourself time to drive to and from your appointments. A rookie mistake in time-blocking I made often during my first few years in real estate is forgetting to schedule drive time, especially if you live somewhere with a lot of traffic. It's always better to give yourself more time than you'll need to ensure you're never late or stressing about being late. The amount of wasted energy that can be avoided by properly blocking time is astonishing. Use this tool to your advantage and avoid unnecessary stress. Also, you won't be your best self if you show up to an appointment while your nervous system is going wild with adrenaline.

Should lead generation activities always happen in the morning? I hear this question all the time. Many of the gurus and other coaches out there will say yes and for good reason. It's common for people to have the most energy in the morning. Studies have shown we have the most willpower in the morning, meaning we are more likely to do the most difficult tasks of the day if we just get them over with rather than waiting until later in the day. And once I start procrastinating, it becomes harder and harder to stop and do the work.

That said, my answer is: It depends. There are many different ways to find business, which we'll go over in Part III of this book, and many of them are socially-based and event-based. None of us can control when the chamber of commerce networking event will happen or when your kid's soccer game is scheduled. So if activities like that are part of your lead gen strategy, chances are they won't fit neatly into a lead gen box each morning from 9-11 a.m. Maybe your lead gen is based on hand-written notes and mailers. I'd be much more inclined to write notes in the evenings while watching *Mad Men* for the fifth time than first thing in the morning. Give yourself grace, do what works for you—what matters most is that the work gets done. The "how" and "when" are much less important. The strategy will vary agent to agent, and we will cover several options for lead generation in the next section.

If you would like to see an example of my own calendar and time blocks from when I was a solo agent, visit www.MoveOverExtroverts.com/Bonus.

Fourteen

Color-Coding

The next step is color-coding your calendar. This is another practice that's quite simple yet powerfully effective. You have probably heard of this concept before, but in case you haven't, here's the gist: You already have your time blocks on your calendar, and it's important to see where exactly you are spending your time. So we create buckets: personal, family, business. Keep personal and family separate; some agents like to combine them, but I advise against it. Introverts need alone time to recharge, so that alone time must be in the calendar. It's not optional.

You can create as many additional buckets as you'd like but definitely no fewer than those core three. You assign each bucket a specific color, and each time-block is color-coded accordingly, either by changing the color in Google calendar or by using highlighters on your paper calendar. Then you can see how you are allocating your time each week.

The purpose behind color-coding your calendar is to ensure the colors are balanced, that you're not spending eighty hours each week working without any family or personal time. (Quick note on family: Family is whatever you define it to be—it doesn't necessarily mean time with children. For me, it's quality time with Keith and Marty).

When I was a solo agent, I used the following colors for my time-blocks:

- Green: Money-making activities. Lead generation, lead follow up, and showings.

- Purple: Listing and buyer appointments. I had a separate color for appointments, so I could quickly scroll through the previous weeks or months and count how many appointments I had gone on for tracking purposes. Visually, it made it so much easier to have a separate color.

- Pink: Me time! I chose my favorite color for my personal time. This included yoga classes, massages, solo trips, and anything I was putting into my calendar for myself. Each week, my goal was to have at least one pink thing on the calendar. If I saw no pink activities for the upcoming week, I'd purposefully add something from my recharge list...

- Blue: Once I launched Move Over Extroverts in 2018, I started using blue as my color for anything MOE related—teaching classes, speaking gigs, coaching sessions with agents. This way, I could see what percentage of my time was spent on real estate and how much I spent on my new coaching business.

Choose your colors and start color-coding your calendar today. Remember: You can change your colors and buckets at any time, so don't worry about getting it "right" the first time around. It's a process, and you'll find what works best for you. The sooner you begin to build your awareness around how you spend your time, the faster you'll be able to control your calendar (versus your calendar controlling you).

Fifteen

Use Your Recharging & Draining Lists Strategically

I've mentioned that there are no magic bullets for most of the advice in this book. However, the concept in this section is pretty darn close. This is where we will be strategic in where we place our time blocks in the calendar and in which order. Hint: You'll want to have your recharge and draining lists handy!

Remember the story I told in the section on dealing with loved ones—the agent who made the small yet significant shift in when he called his family member? I will never forget this conversation and am very grateful to this agent for helping me discover one of my biggest realizations around time and energy management—how to be strategic and purposeful with the order of activities. The order of operations matters so much more than we think it does.

It's safe to say that the listing/buyer appointments are the highest-stakes and most important time-blocks in the calendar. These are crucial hours when we have to be completely focused, confident yet relaxed, and bring our absolute best versions of ourselves to the potential clients' kitchen tables.

Keeping that in mind, you have an incredible opportunity to improve your appointment conversion rates by being more strategic with your time leading up to your appointments. It truly is a simple concept that every agent can implement immediately. It is free and requires no additional skill, only increased awareness and thoughtful intention.

Ask yourself: What activities are proven to replenish my energy? Schedule something from your recharge list right before your appointment. Equally as important, ask yourself: What do I know will drain my energy? Avoid those before your listing and buyer appointments. These are subtle changes, but they can make a massive difference in how you show up to these meetings.

Consider your schedule from the past week. Go back and look through your calendar. Are there any places where changing the order of activities would have made a difference? I'd guess there are at least one or two examples you can find, and that's good. Study, collect data, learn, and improve. This is a process of constantly re-evaluating how you spend your time and energy, making small tweaks along the way.

Sixteen

Take Days Off

Before you call me crazy and skip this chapter, let me assure you it is possible to take days off in real estate. Even as a solo agent, I've done it. I've taught thousands of agents how to do it. And after reading this chapter, you'll have all the tools you need to take regular, consistent days off too.

First, we need to talk about why days off are so important. It's not about the touchy-feely, self-care bubble baths and massages (although those are fantastic). Taking dedicated time to step away from your business allows you to operate at your highest level. Incorporating regular days off into your routine will make you a better real estate agent, a better business owner, and a more healthy, balanced human.

Occasionally, I come across people who believe days off are for the lazy, the weak, the unmotivated, or for people who simply don't want success badly enough. They're wrong. The opposite is true. This practice is for the benefit of yourself and your business.

Imagine a worn out, stressed real estate agent answering the phone at the end of a long day. He's already frustrated because one of his clients decided to rent for another year instead of buying a home, and his annoying younger brother texted again, asking to borrow more money. Oh, and his lunch order was wrong. What a day! He also hasn't taken a single day off in three weeks. Now it's 7:45 p.m., and the co-broke agent on one of his listings is calling to say the inspection results came back, and the buyers are asking for a $30k price reduction.

How do you predict he will handle this news? A well-rested agent would take the call graciously, letting the other agent know he will discuss it with his sellers and get back to him tomorrow, then call the sellers, deliver the news calmly, and talk through the options. Negotiating inspection items is a commonplace part of the job, after all. A frustrated, burned out agent, however, is more likely to have an emotional response. He may not be able to see all the options clearly or communicate them calmly to his clients. I know; I've been that agent. You've likely been that agent at some point in your career. No judgement.

There are two key aspects here:

1. Physical rest. Hopefully, we are all getting enough sleep—the Mayo Clinic and Harvard Health agree that adults most need at least seven hours of high quality sleep each night to be healthy. In a perfect world, days off aren't meant to be used as sleep-catch-up-days, but sometimes, that is the reality. The body needs to be well-rested to function at its best. And the mind and body are more interconnected than most people realize. So you hereby have permission to take all the naps your body needs!

2. Mental rest. This is an even bigger component of a true day off—the space to take a mental break from the stress of this

business. We are in a highly stressful industry; there's no denying it. Yet purposefully taking time away will allow you to have longevity in your real estate career. The mental rest you achieve during your days off gives the brain space to be creative, to think through problems you may be facing, and to provide perspective.

Now that you're convinced days off are essential, let's dive into the practical side of how to take days off as a solo agent (we'll cover teams a bit later). Here's how you do it:

- Find a colleague in your office who you trust and work well with. Don't venture outside of your office, as you may open yourself up to liability that your broker's errors & omissions policy won't cover. Check with your broker to verify.

- Invite your colleague out for coffee and propose a solution to help you both take regular days off. This is *not* a proposal to form a team. It's simply an agreement to cover for each other one or two days per week. If they're amendable, great! You now have coverage for your days off. If they are not interested, ask someone else. No hard feelings.

- Coordinate your days off so you two don't overlap. If the other agent is planning to take Wednesdays off, you take Thursdays off, for instance.

- Decide how you're going to compensate each other. You could charge by the hour for any work done or avoid having to Venmo one another each week by agreeing to no formal compensation—just cover for each other for the equal amount of days and call it even. The latter is cleaner in terms of taxes; this is one consideration to keep in mind.

- Communicate with your clients. Let them know you have a colleague who will take amazing care of them if you're ever not available. Share with them that you'll be unavailable on certain days. Clients only want to know they'll be taken care of and responded to quickly. They usually don't care who responds as long as they are given a heads-up in advance. Better yet, introduce your colleague to your current clients ahead of time.

- Check in with your colleague the following day. Make sure you're staying in the loop on everything that happened during your day off.

- Practice. This will feel incredibly strange at first. You'll feel guilty. You might feel lazy. Push through it, and do not give in to the temptation to check your email or answer texts. If there's a true emergency, your colleague will let you know. It does get easier with practice.

- Start small. Start with just a half day off if a full day seems too daunting at first. Work your way up. The more you see that the business is just fine, the easier this will become.

- Do things to help you shut your brain off. No, I'm not talking about ingesting hallucinogens. I mean reading fiction, watching documentaries, watching trash TV (admit it—you love it too!), or doing hot yoga or your preferred intense physical activity that requires focus.

Now, here's your homework: Go into your calendar and schedule a day off. You can start with just an afternoon if that's more feasible, but block off time to rest your mind and body, away from your business. If you're really up for a challenge, schedule time off every week for the next month. Use what you learned in this chapter to make it happen, and enjoy (guilt-free)! Your business will thank you.

Seventeen

Leverage (in Unexpected Places)

At its core, leverage is simply finding ways to streamline aspects of your life or business to free up time and energy. On any given day, we all have the same number of hours, and it's up to us how we use that time. Think of it like a game of who can use their time the most strategically and impactfully. Leverage is a valuable tool to give yourself an advantage in this game.

When real estate coaches and trainers talk about leverage, they're usually talking about leveraging your time in your business (such as hiring your first assistant). Yes, that's absolutely an important piece of leverage. Other common types of leverage usually discussed are hiring a housekeeper, a landscaper, or a laundry service. All of these are worthwhile, and I'd recommend them. If you've been in real estate for any length of time, you've heard all this before.

I'd like to add to the conversation around leverage with some unexpected places to find and implement it:

- **Create a business plan each year and stick to it.** Business planning is a type of leverage because it saves you from having to constantly make decisions about what activities you'll do. Sit down for a few days and figure out what the next year will look like, how you'll find business (your lead gen plan), and what changes you want to make going forward. Then you're done! You won't have to do this deep, energetically-taxing work again until next year. Following your plan is leverage for your mental energy and your decision-making energy, both of which are finite. Don't deviate from the plan, either. Keep your head down, do the work, and analyze the results the following year. A quarterly check-in to make sure you're on target is advised, but be careful not to let these check-ins completely derail your plan. Instead, use these check-ins as maintenance and make tweaks to improve your conversion rates.

- **Create processes and stick to them.** When you sign a new listing, what's your process? What are your standards for communication? How do you manage paperwork? How do you keep track of all the tasks involved in every transaction? By creating standards and processes for both buyers and sellers, you'll save yourself an incredible amount of time, energy, and stress going forward. The level of customer service you provide will also inevitably improve. Oh, and you'll avoid potential lawsuits that can occur when one client is treated differently than the next. Call me crazy, but I've seen it happen. Creating and documenting these systems is tedious and not easy. However, it's more than worth it, and when you make your first hire, that person can help you organize and refine your processes.

- **Let go of perfectionism.** I've struggled with this and still do sometimes, although it's gotten better over the years. Striving for perfection sounds great in theory, doesn't it? We want to do the best job possible. We never want to make a mistake; we never want to let anyone down or disappoint anyone. That's all very noble, but the reality is this: No one is perfect, and there's a line at which striving to be perfect becomes unhealthy. Here's how you can tell the difference between a healthy desire to be great and a toxic obsession to be perfect: If you make a mistake and learn from it, that's healthy. If you make a mistake and spiral into negative self-talk for days, that's counterproductive (again, this is easier said than done, and I'm guilty of it myself). How does this fit into the leverage section of the book? Negative self-talk can be a massive time and energy drain, so learning how to avoid it will give you back all that time and energy. The shift starts subtly, and it's all in our own minds,—it's our reactions to our mistakes. Focus on learning from every mistake, and you'll turn mistakes into positive experiences. It also helps to take a step back and look at the situation from above. It's human nature to exacerbate issues and lose sight of the big picture. Start practicing the art of looking at every missed opportunity for perfectionism from a bird's eye view, and you'll see that everything will be okay. There's no problem that doesn't have a solution, and when you remain relaxed and level-headed about an issue, you're much more likely to find the best solution.

Eighteen
The Irish Goodbye

Definition: To leave a party, bar, or other social gathering to avoid having to say goodbye to acquaintances at the event. One connotation is that the person leaving is noticeably intoxicated and desires to leave without having to converse with anyone they know and reveal their state of intoxication. Origin: Boston, Massachusetts. Source: Rice University

The Irish goodbye is one of my favorite ways to preserve my energy at the end of a long day. Leaving without saying goodbye works beautifully at a networking event or conference. It can be tricky at an intimate dinner party or if you're the guest in someone's home, but let's focus on using it in the context of a large, loud event where you can easily slip away (don't you love the anonymity of a large event? I sure do).

Energy is a resource, as we now know. So taking the time and spending the energy to make the rounds and say goodbye to everyone before leaving is actually quite an investment. Is it worth it? Every situation will be different, and sometimes there are times when it is indeed worth it. However, most of the time, your energy is better spent elsewhere. The most beneficial way you can spend your energy during an event is in deep conversation one-on-one with a few individuals over the course of the night. A round of goodbyes is just more idle chit-chat, more small talk not worth my time or energy.

If it feels too strange to just walk out the door, a baby step is excusing yourself and going to the restroom first. Then bail. I've done this countless times. Leaving early also gives you a reason to follow up with the people you spoke with the next day, saying, "I didn't get a chance to say goodbye to you last night. Why don't we meet up for coffee next week and continue our conversation?" So the next time you're at an event and want to leave, you officially have permission and encouragement to Irish goodbye!

Nineteen

The Dreaded 20k+ Person Conference

Yes, we introverts do attend conferences and conventions. Some of us dread them. The aggressive club music (oh, sorry, I mean "motivational" music), the over-the-top speaker systems, and the swarm of sleep-deprived yet amped-up people can be completely overwhelming. If you're also a highly sensitive person (HSP), large conferences are even more intense.

Think about the last time you were at a networking event or a conference. There are people everywhere, bright lights, and the loud, ambient noise of meaningless small talk. It's tiring just being there. Then you see someone you want to talk to, but it's too loud to decipher what they're saying. As I write this chapter, I'm at the National Association of Realtors (NAR) convention here in Boston. I've roamed around the convention center for about ten minutes and found a nice, quiet nook to sit and write. I needed a break from "peopleing," and writing a book is as good an excuse as any!

At this point in my career, I've grown to love conferences. I know that's strange to hear from the self-proclaimed queen of the introverts, but it's true. Yet I only love them because I've learned how to tailor the experience through more than a decade of attending conferences of every shape and size. I've been to training classes with a handful of people, full-day classes with a few hundred, smaller conferences of several thousand, and the largest real estate conventions in the world with tens of thousands of people roaming about, fighting for tables at every restaurant in town (if you spotted me at Hooter's in Austin, Texas circa 2015, it was the only place with available seating—I swear!).

Let's focus on the large, national, or international conferences since those are typically the most challenging for us introverts. Here are my favorite strategies for making them not only tolerable but extremely enjoyable and productive, the best possible use of your time:

- **Book your own room.** Your hotel room can serve as your quiet sanctuary, but this only works if you do not have a roommate. Yes, it's more expensive, but it will be worth it when you are craving solitude. The exception is if you're traveling with your spouse or romantic partner; in that case, it might make sense to share.

- **Do not attend everything.** You've likely paid a lot of money to be there, and because of that, it's easy to feel guilty about skipping parts of the conference. It's much more productive to focus on the one or two things that are the most important and skip the rest. Even if you did go to every session, it would be impossible to remember everything you learned, let alone implement it all. By focusing on one or two things, you're more likely to successfully implement what you learned when you get home. And you won't burn yourself out in the process. Give yourself permission to skip sessions, especially if that will free up enough energy to network. Ask yourself: What will be the best investment of my time and energy? Attend those sessions and skip the rest.

- **Plan strategic one-to-one meetings.** Instead of attending every class, use some of your time to schedule one-to-one meetings. These will be quieter and a welcome change of pace from the large sessions. Conferences provide amazing opportunities to meet people you wouldn't normally meet, so take advantage of this. Reach out to a few people you're interested in meeting and invite them to coffee. This way, you'll be making stronger connections with a few rather than meaninglessly swapping business cards with hundreds.

- **Go to bed early, at least some nights.** It's all too easy to get sucked into the after-hours social events, especially if you are friends with your colleagues. While the ideal number of nights in versus nights out will vary from person to person, as a general guideline, plan to get to bed at a decent hour about half of the nights. Trust me—you'll thank yourself in the morning if you aren't out until 3 a.m. every night.

- **Have groceries delivered to your hotel room.** This can be done in advance and is a huge life-saver. You'll save money, save time, and improve your healthy food intake. The biggest benefit is having food readily available and avoiding having to leave your room to forage among the masses. Okay, there's room service, but I find having to wait forty-five minutes for a thirty-dollar bowl of cereal and some fruit to be much more annoying than having it available in my room.

- **Take breaks and find quiet spaces (they do exist).** When you feel overwhelmed by the noise and crowds, allow yourself a break. The benefit to convention centers being so large is that there is always a quiet place to retreat to. All you have to do is find it. I usually have the best luck going up or down a flight of stairs. The secret is bathrooms and hallways. Use these quiet places to take a break from the crowds. If there's a line for the restroom, go find another one. There are usually multiple restrooms on every floor. Walk until you find a quiet spot, and use the time to recharge your energy.

- **Stay in a hotel at or near the convention center**. To that end, my personal favorite quiet retreat place is my hotel room. When I need a break, I love the ease of a quick walk to my room. There have been a few times I've stayed in a hotel many blocks from the convention center, and I always regret it. I feel a little trapped when I can't run back to the room for fifteen minutes of quiet.

- **Ladies, wear comfy shoes.** Comfortable shoes will not only make your entire experience more pleasant, they'll allow you to scoot back to your room without pain. In the past, I've made the mistake of wearing super cute, super uncomfortable stilettos. So by midday, when I need my break, my feet are too sore to walk all the way back to my hotel or to even walk around enough to find a quiet space. Miserable. Guys, you might think this is silly, but the struggle is real.

- **Plan self-care to look forward to.** A massage, a trip to the salon, an awesome new book, dinner alone one night, a first-class upgrade—plan something that you'll enjoy by yourself. Think of it as a mini-vacation while you're on a work trip. My favorite is finding a fantastic restaurant and treating myself to a lovely meal to enjoy with the pleasure of my own company. The first time I was asked to speak on stage at Inman, I splurged on the omakase menu at Nobu in Vegas. Worth every penny.

- **Take guilt-free naps.** Seriously. Plenty of naps, zero guilt.

- **Clear your schedule when you get home.** Plan time to recover for a day or two when you get home. Set that expectation ahead of time with anyone who needs to know that you need rest.

Heather Schmidt, a Keller Williams agent in Chicago, shares her experiences attending conferences as both an introvert and an empath:

> "I remember my first Family Reunion convention—I packed my calendar, running from breakout room to breakout room back to the main stage, ALL DAY LONG. I did not have any time to myself and went

straight to an evening event. Once there, I could not handle being hugged. When someone was loud/excited, I cringed. I called my husband in tears from complete sensory overload. I forced myself to stay for about an hour and realized I was not serving myself or others, so I left. Walking back to the hotel by myself, I immediately felt relief. I now make sure to build in white space and give myself time to recharge. Also, giving myself permission to NOT ATTEND ALL THE THINGS has been HUGE."

Heather Schmidt

Twenty
Solo Vacations

We've talked about the importance of days off, and once you master that, the next level is taking a solo vacation. I know this isn't for everyone, but it's a great way to maximize your time and reset your mind. The beauty of a solo trip is you can do whatever you want, whenever you want. You don't spend any time having conversations about what you're going to do, where you'll eat, or when you'll go to bed each night. Yes, vacations with family and romantic vacations with partners are amazing and wonderful. Yet they're not always the most relaxing. Sometimes they are but not always. A solo vacation is just you, so you can make it as relaxing or adventurous as you choose.

Spend time with yourself. Your brain will reap the same benefits as it does when you take days off, only much more so. You can go somewhere local—a solo vacation doesn't have to be a week alone in Aruba or a Mediterranean cruise (although I've done both and can't recommend them enough). One night in a hotel an hour from your home can be extremely beneficial and a productive use of time. The change in environment does something unique to the body and mind.

Aside from calling it a "reset," I struggle to put the experience into words, which I know is not ideal for my book. You may have to just trust me on this one and try it for yourself. I'd love to hear your thoughts afterwards! Email me at Ashley@MoveOverExtroverts.com with your solo vacation stories or post them on IG and tag me.

Take Action:

- Add time-blocks in your calendar for the next month.

- Color-code your calendar for the next month.

- Go through your calendar each week and look for opportunities to change the order of your activities. Set a reminder, so you don't forget.

- Schedule your days off throughout the next month. Aim for at least one per week.

- Create a strategic plan for the next conference you attend.

- Consider planning a solo vacation, even just for a weekend or one night away!

Part III

Lead Generation

Finesse Literary Press Ltd.

Part III

"Here's the advantage in sales we introverts have over our extroverted peers: We don't rely on our personality. In the absence of natural talent, we have to rely on a process...and in the long-run, process beats personality. Every time."

Matthew Pollard, The Introvert's Edge

Twenty-One
A Mindset Shift

Before we dive into specific tactics to find more clients, we have to talk about the mindset shift all real estate agents need to have at some point in their careers. I've seen it with the thousands of agents I've recruited, trained, and coached. It's the shift from "lead generation is bothering people and selling them something" to "lead generation is looking for more people who need my help." Your job each day is to go out and find those people who want or need to buy or sell real estate. That's it! We are never trying to convince people to move; that's not our job. We simply find people who have a real estate need, provide them guidance and information, and help them achieve their goals. No pressure, no hard-selling. We are here as resources whenever someone is ready to move based on what's happening in their life.

This shift will make it easier to talk to people about real estate because you'll be more excited about it, and you'll bring a different energy to each conversation. Everyone you talk to will pick up on that new energy, even if they aren't aware of it. Most of us are hyper-aware that the public generally perceives us as sleazy, used car salespeople. The NAR lawsuits certainly haven't helped our image either. To combat this perception, adopt this new mindset and go out into the world with it. Real estate is about helping people get what they want, not convincing anyone to do something they don't want to do. We are consultants, not salespeople.

There are only two situations in real estate when we truly function as salespeople: when we're presenting our value proposition to a prospective client (selling ourselves) and when we're the listing agent on a property (selling the property). That's it. Everything else we do is consulting, marketing, and negotiating, with a healthy dose of psychology.

Knowing this truth should make it easier to talk to people about real estate. Memorizing and repeating the previous few sentences can quickly disarm a skeptical lead who's worried you're going to try to talk them into buying a house they don't want or selling their family home before they're ready. It will help you build trust quickly, which will allow you to deepen the relationship, receive a referral, or help this lead with something real estate related. I've received plenty of referrals during my career because I was not the pushy salesperson.

Twenty-Two

Choose Your Niche

"The riches are in the niches." Trite but true. A niche is a specific type of buyer or seller you choose to work with. Some common niches are: first-time home buyers, investors, downsizers, waterfront properties, luxury properties, land, commercial, farms, and vacation/second homes. If you're wondering why an agent would want to limit themselves to just one niche, let me explain.

The purpose of choosing a niche is to increase your odds of receiving referrals and being your sphere's go-to real estate agent. It's counter-intuitive, but focusing on one niche will help your network think of you when a real estate need arises for them or for someone they know. It taps into a very cool brain function called the Reticular Activating System or RAS. A blog post written by BNI New Zealand explains it well:

> "The Reticular Activating System or RAS is a bundle of nerves that sits in your brainstem. And its job is to regulate behavioural consciousness and motivation. It

> filters out unnecessary information, so the important stuff gets through. The RAS is the reason you learn a new word and then start hearing it everywhere or buy a new car and start noticing them everywhere."
>
> BNI New Zealand

Agents can absolutely specialize in a specific niche and choose to only work with those clients, but most agents I know are more than happy to work with clients outside of their niche. Your neighbor might say, "Hey, I know you work mostly with first-time buyers, but would you be interested in selling our house and helping us find something larger?" Then you can decide what to do. Chances are, you'll probably say, "Yes, of course. I'd be thrilled to work with you!"

Now, let's say you specialize in working with first-time buyers and your neighbor says, "I'm thinking about buying an apartment building to add to my real estate portfolio. Could you help?" If you don't have any commercial or investment experience, you may want to refer that piece of business to an agent who will better serve the client. Either way, you want every lead coming to you, so you can decide whether to work with each client or refer them to someone else. The more leads, the better, regardless of the specifics.

The brain works better with specifics. If I ask you if you know anyone who's thinking about buying a car, you'd likely say no. But if I ask you if you know any parents who have a teenager and might be in the market for a used car for the newest driver in their family, chances are someone just came to mind. Generically asking your database if they know anyone who's looking to buy or sell real estate isn't nearly as effective as asking if they have any friends or co-workers who are complaining about their rent going up or their landlord being annoying and might want to talk about buying a home. Help them refer business to you.

There's a successful agent in Florida named Michael Heissenbuttel whose niche is working with older people. He has brilliantly built an entire brand around this niche ("Your Grandma's Realtor"), and it's so memorable that he gets calls for all types of real estate needs, not just selling grandmothers' houses. Here's what he says:

> "Being 'Your Grandma's Realtor' has largely helped me in two ways: First, it made me memorable. In a sea of thousands of Realtors, there are dozens of Michaels, even more tall white brunettes, but only one Grandma's Realtor. Second, it associates me with important values. When someone thinks of a good Realtor for Grandma, they'd think of someone who is patient, a good listener, and cares about more than just closing the transaction. When people remember me that way, it doesn't matter if it's a grandma or not, I'll be their first call."
>
> Michael Heissenbuttel

So choose a niche you'd like to work, and then market the heck out of it. You will not be limited to only working with those types of clients, and you'll make it easier for everyone you know to remember you and send you referrals.

Twenty-Three
Use Your Joy List

Back in section one, you created your Joy List. If you skipped that activity, I'd recommend going back to the Joy List chapter and completing the exercise or at least starting to jot down some items to begin your list. It's very simple—what brings you joy? This list is useful for managing your energy by strategically incorporating joyful items into your calendar to purposefully increase your positive energy. It's also an incredibly useful starting point when deciding which lead generation activities you'll focus on. Out of the hundreds of possible tactics to find business, choosing ones that you enjoy doing (or at least don't hate and dread) is the key to sticking with them and seeing success.

Now, I've seen highly successful real estate agents grow their businesses by doing activities they didn't enjoy at first, and that's okay. It's to be expected. In the beginning of any real estate agent's career, every activity will be new, unfamiliar, and even scary. Even the experienced agents I've coached experience fear and uncertainty when they implement a new strategy. It's normal, and it's okay. Be sure not to fall into the common trap of discounting a strategy solely because it's uncomfortable at first.

Let's take one of my favorite activities as an example—yoga. Yes, you may love attending your weekly yoga class, but striking up conversations with other yogis in your class may be terrifying. Maybe you want to keep yoga on your joy list and not turn it into a lead gen activity, so it remains purely a time to relax. Or maybe you regularly chat with your fellow students before or after class anyway, and telling them you're working in real estate is a perfectly natural topic of conversation. Maybe you start with just wearing a real estate related or company branded tank top to class and see if anyone asks you about it. With every hobby or activity, you have options. You can keep each hobby as a purely joyful activity or turn it into a lead gen strategy. Both options are wonderful and serve a purpose. Think about what sounds like the best option for you, try it out, assess both the results and how you feel, and adjust accordingly.

You may think I'm contradicting myself, but let me explain further. Time and effort are key. Every strategy will feel uncomfortable at first. We know this, and there's no getting around it. So when you're considering which strategies to implement to find business, choose several. Choose at least one that's rooted in your joy list. Choose at least one that's proven to work and has systems around it you can implement. That balance is important. Here's why: The joyful activity, when used as a lead generation tool, might still be new and potentially scary. Give each one a fair shot before discounting it. Six months to one year is typically enough time to accurately gauge results from any lead gen activity. Use your Joy List as a starting point to lean into activities that you already enjoy. This will make the act of finding new clients much more pleasant.

Twenty-Four

Hobbies, Charity, Groups, and Clubs

In addition to your Joy List, think about your hobbies, any charities you're involved in, groups you're a member of, or clubs you belong to. You can turn these into lead generation by being more purposeful in your attendance and the nature of your conversations.

Let's say you already belong to a book club. It meets once a month, but you attend only a few times per year. Everyone else talks about their work, but you tend to stay quiet to not come off as a pushy real estate agent. How would you turn your membership in this club into a consistent lead gen activity? A few subtle yet powerful changes could have a big impact:

1. Make it a priority to attend every month. This will keep you top of mind with the other members and help you deepen your relationships with them faster. Consistency is key.

2. Talk about real estate—not in an annoying, salesy way, but in

a friendly, conversational way. Telling stories is the best way to talk about real estate in a social environment.

Storytelling is my secret weapon for talking about real estate in any social setting. People are fascinated by real estate—we know this because there are entire TV networks and top-rated shows about our industry. There are celebrity real estate agents walking the red carpet! Imagine binge-watching a Netflix show about selling life insurance. There are very few industries as seemingly glamorous and sexy as real estate, though we know much of what we see isn't an accurate portrayal. The point is the public loves real estate. This is a very good thing for us. Use it.

When you strike up a conversation with someone, look for ways to tell a quick, engaging story about real estate. It can be about a client situation (keep it anonymous, of course), a property you toured recently, or a story another agent shared with you. Keep it short and to the point. If you can add humor, that would be even better. Here are a few examples, each of which would be appropriate in response to someone asking, "How are you?":

- "I'm great! We had a few offers on this condo I'm selling, and we've been going back and forth to get the highest price for the seller. We just accepted an amazing offer today, and my client is so happy."

- "I'm exhausted but good! I spent the morning in a dingy basement from the 1880s at a home inspection. I think I still have cobwebs in my hair! Then I showed a few houses to another buyer before coming here."

- "I'm doing well! One of my neighbors referred me to her parents, who are moving to the new retirement community being built in town. They have a lot of stuff in their house, so I'm introducing them to one of my organizers, who will help them purge and pack over the next few months. It's always great to be brought in early in the process, so I can make sure they're working with the best people and are taken care of."

Notice I never said the word "busy." This is very important. The danger in saying you're busy is that people may assume you're too busy to take great care of any referrals they send you. So avoid that word at all costs (it's also expected, boring, and adds no value to a conversation). In her book *The Mountain is You*, philosopher Brianna Wiest writes: "…being 'busy' is not a virtue; it only signals to others that you do not know how to manage your time or your tasks." Let's remove that word from our vocabulary entirely.

It's also critical to stay positive, upbeat, and authentic. No one wants to hear a professional complain, yet if you're trying too hard to put a good spin on a bad situation, it will come off as phony. Then you'll lose credibility. If you had a great day, share it without coming off as arrogant (most of us introverts usually don't run the risk of being arrogant). If you had a terrible day, be honest without going too far into detail, and end with something optimistic. Example: "It's been a rough day. Glad it's over, and I can relax now. Tomorrow's a new day!"

Know your audience. If you're attending an evening PTA meeting, think of a story to tell that involves a fellow parent or a client who has a young family. Make it as relatable as possible. This will trigger the person's RAS, and they'll subconsciously think about how you could help them or other families they know.

Any place you're regularly around the same group of people is an opportunity to build relationships and find real estate clients directly or through referral. Go through your calendar from the past few months and see where you're spending time with people. Any hobby, charity, group, or club counts. Then decide if you'd like to lean into any of these and turn them into lead generation. You're already going to be there anyway—why not become the real estate agent of choice?

You also have the benefit of a controversial phenomenon called "in-group bias." This concept is explained in detail in an article written by Dr. Sekoul Krastev and Dan Pilat:

> *"In-group bias* (also known as in-group favoritism) is the tendency for people to give preferential treatment to others who belong to the same group that they do. This bias shows up even when people are put into groups randomly, making group membership effectively meaningless."
>
> Dr. Sekoul Krastev and Dan Pilat

While this bias has the potential to lead to negative outcomes, it can be positive in business. Commonality builds trust. Think about this the next time you're at a sports bar and the person next to you is cheering for the same team, perhaps the New England Patriots anytime before 2023. Have you ever seen someone in an airport reading the book you just finished or met a stranger on vacation who happens to be from your hometown? These commonalities create bonds between people, even if they are arbitrary. Using this reality to foster deeper relationships may be considered a bit opportunistic, but it is also a shrewd business strategy.

Twenty-Five

Housewarming Parties

Hosting housewarming parties for buyers is one of my favorite lead generation strategies. It's a better use of money than a traditional closing gift because it's a way to meet new potential clients (and you can usually write off the entire amount you spend since it's a marketing expense, but double-check with your CPA). Some buyers won't want one, and that's okay. It's an option. I like to tease it at my initial buyer consultation to plant the seed and to get their reaction to see if they're interested or not.

If your buyer does want a housewarming party, here's how to do it:

- **Set a date and time.** Most buyers will want some time to move and settle in before having a party in their new home, so coordinate with them on timing. Weekends are best, but you could host one on a weeknight. Let the buyers decide, as it'll be hosted in their home and with their circle of friends.

- **Send out the invitations.** Electronic invitations are easier and cheaper than paper invites, so I'd recommend using Paperless Post or Evite. Ideally, your clients will give you their guest list and contact information for everyone, then you can send out the invitations on their behalf. Some clients prefer to handle the invites themselves, which is fine, too.

- **Arrange for refreshments.** Tell your buyers you'll take care of the food and ask them what they'd like. You can give some suggestions to guide them to your desired price point, such as "Pizza and salad tend to be crowd-pleasers" or "Let's make this a show-stopping event. Do you like sushi?" Consider partnering with a vendor to split the cost. Perhaps reach out to the loan officer or closing attorney/title company who did the deal with you.

- **Host the event!** Show up early to get everything set up, and be sure you meet everyone who attends. Chances are, the buyers will introduce you to their friends and sing your praises. Stick around after to clean up, and be sure to congratulate your buyers one more time on their new home purchase.

- **Follow up.** If anyone at the party is thinking about buying a house, this is a perfect opportunity for them to talk to you about it. Then you can follow up and set up a consultation with them. Follow up with everyone via email to thank them for coming, and offer to help anyone else who has a real estate need.

MOVE OVER EXTROVERTS

Hosting parties can be exhausting, especially for us introverts. Use your energy management skills to make sure you are at your best energy level going into the event, and use your time management skills to book yourself plenty of rest afterwards. It will be draining. That's okay. It will be worth it when you pick up a new client or two.

Twenty-Six

Client Appreciation Events

Some of us are much better in person than over the phone (I'm one of them). Hosting client appreciation events is another great way to get face-to-face with people, thank them for their business/referrals/support, and encourage more referrals in the future. They also help agents stay top of mind. When you see an old friend in person, you think about that person much longer than if they merely sent you an email. The same is true for all humans. In his book *The 7 Levels of Communication*, Michael J. Maher ranks 1:1 meetings and events/seminars at the top of his Communication Pyramid, meaning they are the most impactful methods of communication (and I highly recommend reading his book and joining his Facebook group "Generosity Generation with Michael J. Maher" to learn more about building a referral-based business).

The time and energy management strategies we talked about in the previous chapter apply here as well. Client events are incredibly draining. You'll be speaking with a lot of people at once, everyone wanting your attention, plus you'll feel the pressure of making sure the event goes well. Plan accordingly. For example, I wouldn't attend any other events or have any meetings the day of the event. Work from home if you can, and minimize your interactions with others as much as possible. This will preserve your energy. There's nothing worse than spending months planning to be drained the day of the event (I speak from experience here).

To plan your event, think about what your people would enjoy doing. Are they mostly couples who love a night out? Families with young kids who may enjoy a daytime activity? Also consider what you'll enjoy! Think about your brand and how your clients perceive you. Whether you realize it or not, people are constantly forming an idea about who we are. They see what we post online, how we dress and speak, and how we promote our businesses. Don't overthink this, but it's something to be aware of.

Here are some ideas, all of which I've personally done successfully with my clients:

- **Take everyone to the movies.** You don't need to rent the whole theater in its entirety—just one screen. Give everyone a voucher for a soda and popcorn, and choose a movie that's appropriate for the audience. This is a great option for the winter months if you're in a cold climate since it's indoors. I also love this idea because it leverages your energy in a big way. You say hi to everyone and goodbye/thanks for coming, but other than those limited interactions, you don't have a lot of conversational heavy-lifting to do. Everyone's busy watching the movie!

- **Host a casual happy hour.** This low-key option gives your guests the flexibility to stop by when they can and stay as long as they wish. I would definitely stick to weeknights for this type of event. Bars and restaurants are more likely to accommodate a large group on a Monday or Tuesday night than on a Thursday or Friday. It's also super easy to plan: Pick a date, find a bar/restaurant with enough space and parking, invite your people, show up, buy a few appetizers to share, buy everyone a drink, and network. No setup or cleanup required. This one does require more energy output, as it's constant chit-chat for a few hours. Be sure to manage your energy accordingly, with plenty of rest before and after the event.

- **Go apple picking.** This is easier if you live in a climate with four seasons, but you could swap this out for strawberry picking or a similar outdoor activity. It's perfect for the whole family and not terribly expensive. Apple picking is a fun seasonal activity. It's something many people will plan to do once a year anyway, so it's a client appreciation event that people truly appreciate! You could host apple picking annually, so your sphere can look forward to each year. Think of it as a signature event.

- **House party.** If your personal residence is large enough (and you don't mind filling it with people), you can host a party at your own house for your clients. The theme can vary: holiday party, Superbowl party, summer BBQ, or Halloween costume party. You can get creative here. The pros: no cost for the venue, a more intimate environment, which will create a closer bond with everyone who attends, and you won't have to drive anywhere. The cons: You would be responsible for setup, cleanup, and catering. Some agents prefer to keep some emotional distance between their clients and themselves (absolutely no judgment). If that's the case, skip the house party, and meet everyone at a restaurant instead.

- **Micro-events.** Over the past few years, I've seen some real estate agents have tremendous success hosting micro-events. These are smaller gatherings of ten to twenty people. Having a smaller group allows you to spend more time with each person and have deeper conversations. It also can create connections among the attendees, further adding to the value you brought the group. Some ideas are: an intimate dinner party at a nice restaurant (pricey), a spa day (pricey), a group hike (free!), or mini-golf (moderately priced). I'd limit these to your VIPs—people who are repeat clients or have sent you multiple referrals.

A common objection I hear to the idea of hosting client events is "I don't have enough past clients to have an event." You don't need a past client list of hundreds to use client events as a fantastic lead generation tool. Invite your friends, current clients, hot leads, neighbors, vendor partners, people you've met at networking events, or partner with another real estate agent you trust and host a combined event. Not every event needs to be huge. Smaller events are just as worthwhile.

Lastly, the number of people who attend your event is not the key metric of success, contrary to what people tend to think. The time and energy you spend inviting people is where the magic happens. Making your sphere of influence and clients feel valued and important matters. Focus on the activity of inviting, rather than stressing out about who shows up. There's a great opportunity to follow up with everyone afterward, either to thank them for coming or to say you missed them and hope they'll be able to attend your next event.

Twenty-Seven
Cold Calling Expired Listings and FSBOs

I know, I know. What's a section about cold calling expired listings and for sale by owners doing in the book for introverts? It may surprise you to hear that a handful of introverts I've worked with really enjoy cold calling. They find it easier to talk to strangers than to approach their families and friends about real estate. If this resonates with you, cold calling might be your new secret weapon. With practice comes confidence, and that will lead to your results.

I'm not one of those people. I tried it, and it's not for me. I'm much better in person. However, unless you've tried it, you don't know. Maybe you are the next cold calling master. My advice is to give it a try. If you see zero results and hate it, it's okay to stop, but give it a fair shot. It's a tried and true standard in real estate sales for a reason. Of course, be sure to follow all TCPA rules to avoid getting fined.

Twenty-Eight
Direct Mail

Sending snail mail is a very introvert-friendly way to prospect for business. You are reaching people in a way that puts them in control of the communication; they are calling or texting you if they want to engage in a conversation. Sending direct mail at scale can also get expensive, so it's key to be strategic in who you're mailing to and your messaging. Here are the best ways to find business using mailers:

- **Send letters to new expired listings.** These can be typed, but I would handwrite the address and sign each one. Acknowledge that their house didn't sell, offer value about how you can help, and include a call to action like "Call/text me if you'd like to chat about a different marketing plan to get your home sold."

- **Send letters to old expired listings.** Going back through old expireds from one or two years ago is an underutilized tactic. It takes some time to research and make sure they didn't end up selling, but it's worth it. These sellers were unsuccessful the first time around, and maybe they're thinking about selling now. Tweak the language of this letter to say you know they were trying to sell their home awhile back, and ask them to call you if they're still interested in selling.

- **"Just sold" postcards.** Sending a postcard to advertise your recently sold listing to the surrounding neighbors is smart, especially when you include any public details about the sale, such as the sale price. People are curious and will want to know what their neighbor's house sold for. Include a call to action, offering an expert pricing analysis on their home.

- **Farm your neighborhood.** Janine Sasso, one of the top agents in the Chicago area, built her entire business using direct mail. She's also a published author and founder of *The Hyper Local Agent*. Here's her advice:

"You've probably heard it said a hundred times: Everything works in real estate. Cold calling works. Door-knocking works. Networking works. But here's the truth they often leave out: Not everything will work for everyone—and it doesn't have to. By now, as you've explored the insights in this book, you've likely realized that your success lies in finding what aligns with you. Alignment is the magic word. As an introvert, I learned that this alignment could transform not only my business but also how I viewed my role as a real estate agent.

When I began my career, I had no sphere of influence in my market. To top it off, I was a full-time parent to two tiny humans who demanded most of my waking hours. This felt like a triple whammy against my success: introverted, no sphere, and limited time. Yet what I saw as obstacles turned out to be blessings in disguise. Being an introvert wasn't a handicap; it was my superpower.

Introverts often excel as business owners because we have a knack for creating systems that work for us. For me, that system was direct mail. Let me take you on a journey through how I discovered my groove in real estate marketing, starting with postcards—a method that gave me the freedom to grow my business while staying true to myself.

Discovering Alignment Through Direct Mail

Early on, open houses became a lifeline for me. I liked them because they flipped the usual dynamic: People came to me instead of me chasing them. My first foray into print marketing happened when I decided to invite neighbors to an open house with a flyer. It was a small, simple step, but it sparked an idea. What if I could create more of these touchpoints without constantly showing up in person?

I started exploring ways to stay connected with past clients. At first, I tried the typical advice:

Quarterly calls to discuss "FORD" topics (family, occupation, recreation, dreams). But honestly? It felt forced, and I dreaded the commission-breath moment when I'd ask, "Do you know anyone looking to buy or sell?"

Quarterly pop-bys with gifts. Nice in theory, but costly and time-intensive—not sustainable for long-term growth.

Social media engagement. While helpful, it required more time as my client base grew. Plus, not everyone was on social media.

The "aha" moment came when my brokerage introduced a sphere-of-influence (SOI) postcard program. It was simple: twelve pre-designed postcards sent monthly to my contact list. Suddenly, I had a system that worked for me, even when I wasn't actively working. This approach preserved my energy while allowing me to grow my business consistently. Over time, I refined my strategies and even began helping other agents use postcards to transform their businesses.

Why Postcards Work for Introverts

Postcards became my secret weapon for another two key aspects of real estate: listing marketing and lead generation.

Listing Marketing

Every agent knows a strong listing marketing plan is essential. For me, postcards became a cornerstone of that plan. Here's why:

Longevity: Unlike a fleeting social media post, postcards often stick around. I've had future sellers contact me years after receiving one of my mailers.

Brand Building: Consistent mailings in a hyperlocal area establish name recognition. Neighbors begin to associate your name with real estate without you having to knock on doors or perform TikTok dances.

Social Proof: Highlighting past successes builds credibility and trust. Sellers see evidence of your expertise right in their mailboxes.

Postcards offered a way to become part of the dinner-table conversation without being intrusive. This subtle yet powerful approach is an introvert's dream: making an impact while staying behind the scenes.

Lead Generation

If your business isn't growing, it's dying. But as an introvert, I needed a lead-generation strategy that didn't leave me drained. Enter postcards.

I started small, delivering flyers by hand. While effective, it wasn't scalable. Then came the breakthrough: automating my mailings. With one click, I could reach hundreds of people. Postcards allowed me to attract leads without cold calling, door-knocking, or facing rejection in person. Prospects reached out to me instead, making the process feel natural and manageable.

Closing Thoughts

Direct mail gave me the leverage I needed to grow my business while staying true to my introverted nature. If you're ready to explore this strategy, start small. Build a list of your sphere or target neighborhood, and send consistent, value-driven postcards. Let your strengths as an introvert guide you. Remember, you don't have to change who you are to succeed in real estate—you just need to align your methods with your personality."

Janine Sasso

For more insights, check out *Success with Real Estate Mailers*, *Success with Just Listed & Just Sold Postcards*, or *Success with Sphere & Past Client Postcards* at www.TheHyperLocalAgent.com.

Twenty-Nine

Open Houses (Part 1)

Old-school? Yes. Effective? Yes. I fall into the camp of believing open houses do sell houses and are great ways to find new buyers and sellers. The energetic toll of open houses can vary greatly, depending on how busy the open house is. Sometimes, not a soul will come through, while other times, the police will show up because there are too many people on the street. I've experienced both and everything in between.

Each agent handles the open house attendee interaction differently. You do what works for you. My personal style is fairly laid back. I know most buyers do not want a pushy agent following them around the house. They're more comfortable when they are free to roam around at their leisure and have private conversations about their likes and dislikes. Buyers feeling comfortable and not pressured are important aspects of not only selling the house but also building rapport with potential clients.

Some of my favorite questions to ask during an open house are:

- Have you already hired a buyer's agent to represent you?

- If they say yes: Great! Please write down their name and company so I can follow up with them and not bother you. Take a look around and let me know what you think.

- If they say no: Okay, no problem! Take a look around and let me know what you think of the house.

- Any questions I can answer about the house?

- Any feedback I can give the sellers, things you loved or anything you didn't like?

If a buyer does not have an agent, you'll want to use the opportunity to build as much rapport with them as you possibly can while they're at the house. Ask questions like:

- Have you been looking for a while, or are you just starting your search?

- Are you renting, or do you own your home currently?

- Tell me about what you're looking for in your ideal home.

- What's your timeline?

Then close for an appointment if the conversation is going well. Offer value first, then ask when you could meet for a buyer consultation: "I'd love to learn more about what you're looking for since I have access to a lot of properties that are not on the market, and one might be the right fit for you. When would you have time to get together?" If they're first-time buyers, offer to take them through the entire buyer process from start to finish during your meeting, so they are better prepared to be out shopping for homes.

As with all lead generation strategies, working open houses requires a solid follow up system. Many buyers who attend open houses are early in their searches, which means more follow-up is required. Don't let that deter you. Simply create a good system for keeping in touch. Keep reading and you'll find a chapter on follow-up later in the book.

Thirty

Community Charity Drives

This brilliant concept is a way to give back to your community and build a name for yourself at the same time. Top agent Ryan Smith in Ontario shares his strategy with us:

> "We've discovered a game-changing way to grow our database, build genuine connections, and make a massive impact in our community—without feeling pushy or "salesy." Our food drives don't just bring people together for a good cause—they position us as local leaders, create powerful conversations, and open doors to real estate opportunities in a way that feels authentic and natural. In our last drive, over eighty participants came together, raising more than 1,200 pounds of food while we booked two real estate ap-

pointments—just by giving back. The best part? It's incredibly simple, low-cost, and works perfectly for introverts because it focuses on service, not self-promotion.

The porch pick-up style keeps the process easy, efficient, and impactful with minimal work. Here's how we do it: Most participants sign up through door knocking, where we have friendly, genuine conversations. About seventy-five percent of those we speak with sign up on the spot. To ensure we reach more people, we also leave behind a postcard directing them to a free Google Form for easy registration, helping us connect with even more homes in the area.

We typically promote the drive three weeks out, giving the community time to prepare while allowing us enough time to door knock effectively. A reminder email goes out the day before collection with simple instructions to leave donations visible from the road for easy porch pick-up. If someone doesn't have email, we follow up with a quick call to ensure they're ready. Any special instructions, like alternative drop-off spots, get tracked in a spreadsheet to keep the process smooth.

On collection day, we personally gather the donations from each home, and afterward, we handwrite and deliver thank-you cards to every participant, leaving a lasting impression. The results are then shared in our newsletter and social media, celebrating the total amount raised and highlighting the community's generosity.

What makes this strategy so effective is the series of meaningful touchpoints it creates: The initial door knock, postcard follow-up, reminder before the event, collection day interaction, personalized thank-you cards, public celebration, and long-term follow-up once participants are added to our database. It's an authentic, non-salesy way to build trust, stay top of mind, and create real estate opportunities—making it perfect for introverts who want to grow their business while making a real difference."

Ryan Smith

Smith also runs the Local Expert Academy; you can check out his training and resources for agents here: www.localexpertacademy.com.

Thirty-One

Starting & Controlling the Conversation

Beginning a conversation about real estate is one of the most intimidating aspects of lead generating. It's where agents tend to freeze. "What do I say?" It will vary depending on who you're talking to and where you are, but here are a few ways to start the conversation:

- **Ask, "What do you do for work?"** When meeting someone new, this easy question allows them to share something about themselves. Then they'll ask you the same question. Now you have an invitation to talk about real estate!

- **Tell a story.** We talked about how to tell real estate stories in social settings in a previous chapter. You can lead into a story with "I saw the craziest thing today" or "Oh man, I have to tell you what happened today." Then tell your story with enthusiasm and engage the person you're talking to.

Keep in mind that every lead generation conversation is simply looking for more people to help buy, sell, or invest in real estate. That's it. It does not need to be scary, and you're not selling anything. You're here to help those who want or need your help. Let this mindset permeate every conversation and influence your energy.

Once you're in the conversation, chances are the person you're talking to will ask you what you think of the current market. That's by far the most common question I get asked whenever someone first learns I work in real estate. There are several ways to answer this. Some coaches say you should turn it around on them and say, "Why do you ask?" to determine whether they're a potential buyer or seller. I find that a little aggressive although I do believe it works.

I answer that question with a positive yet vague statement, such as, "It's still a strong seller's market, and every market is good for someone!" Then I follow it up with a specific story about a recent sale to prove I'm knowledgeable and successful as a producing agent. Example: "We're not seeing the frenzy of twenty-plus offers on every house like we were a few years ago, but we just listed a house last week and received multiple offers on it." If they ask about buyers getting offers accepted, I tell a success story about finding a buyer for an off-market property. In this way, I'm able to control the conversation and tell the story I want to tell.

Every real estate story you tell should share a lesson without you having to come out and say it. Use the implied lessons to your advantage, and be strategic. Which lesson do you want to share? Is it that you're a strong listing agent in any market or that you're an expert in finding properties for your buyers that other buyers don't have access to? You get to choose.

I'm writing this just months after the August 2024 NAR lawsuits around buyer agent compensation. Because this was so highly publicized in the news yet not covered in a way the general public can understand, I've gotten a lot of questions about it. "How are you navigating the changes?" "What do you think about the lawsuits?" "I heard many agents will be getting out of the business—is that true?" I absolutely love these questions! They give me an opportunity to control the narrative while showcasing my expertise.

My response: "For us, it's business as usual. The good agents have been using buyer agency agreements with every client all along. That's how we were trained. I've always had a one to two hour consultation with every buyer, and they hired me before we started working together. If a buyer doesn't want to hire me, that's perfectly fine—I wish them well, but I don't work for free. These lawsuits will force the unprofessional agents to treat this like the business it is although it's really unfortunate that the people who will suffer in the end are the first-time and lower income buyers." People are stunned. They don't expect this level of nuance in an answer, probably because they've had the same conversation with multiple real estate agents and only heard fear and outrage. At least, that's my perception based on what I've heard my colleagues saying.

The point is this: You can control the conversation. Be prepared for the handful of likely questions and know what you want to say and how you want to be perceived. If your confidence isn't there or you're earlier in your career, practice in the car. The more you say your answer to "How's the market?" out loud, the easier it will roll off your tongue when you're in conversation with someone else. You could also practice with your spouse, your coach, the colleague who covers your days off, or your cat!

> "I have learned after years in real estate that the easiest calls to make are to people you know to not necessarily talk about real estate with the hard sell but to just keep in touch. These calls are ones I can make for an hour or two each day sustainably. If you want me to call angry expired leads, it will take me all day just to call two of them and work up the energy to do it.
>
> I have built my entire business around my database and serving them at a high level. I have lots of automation built into the touch campaign, and each touch is thoughtfully done to make the database feel as connected to me as I can. There is some forced intimacy with one of our newsletters that gives insights into our family, which I may not normally share openly on the phone. They can bring these topics up, and I am happy to continue to build and strengthen that relationship during the conversation.
>
> Being thoughtful about your business and how marketing interweaves with your prospecting is what creates sustainability. Sustainability is what introverts need, so when energy may be down one day, the

systems and connectivity are still being strengthened even if the phone calls are not necessarily being made."
Chelsea Anderson

Thirty-Two
Navigating Networking Events

Networking events are amazing tools for making new connections, strengthening existing relationships, and staying top of mind as a real estate professional in your community. For us introverts, though, they can be less than appealing at times, especially if you are new to networking.

First, let's discuss networking groups. Common types of groups are: chambers of commerce, referral groups like BNI, women's groups, young professional groups, or industry-specific networking groups, such as your local REALTOR association group. There are all sorts of groups, each with its own specific mission; however, the main purpose is to bring business professionals together. Simple as that. The process of finding the groups that work best for you begins with research and ends with experimentation. There is no way around the trial and error phase. You'll be able to eliminate some groups based on factors such as timing, location, or cost, but you'll also have to visit many groups to narrow it down and choose the best options for you. In my experience, this can be a somewhat arduous process, yet it's very much worth the effort. And as always, trust your gut. The individuals and the leadership are the most important aspects of the group.

The most common timing for networking events are: breakfast meetings, lunch meetings, and after hours events. Breakfast and lunch meetings are typically more structured. There may be a formal round of introductions, and it's smart to have a quick elevator pitch ready to go (another thing to practice in your car or with your spouse/cat). After hours events are usually more relaxed and casual. People are winding down from work, having a cocktail, and loosening up. Pro tip: Bring cash, as it's often a cash-only bar, especially if the event is in a hotel and not a restaurant.

When you attend a group's event for the first time, here is what to expect and how to handle it: Many of the people there will likely know each other already, so there's the potential for the group to seem "cliquey." While some may be, most groups simply have a core group of regular attendees who have become friends over the years. Don't let that scare you away. If you know someone else who will be attending, plan to meet them there at a predetermined time. You two can approach others together, which always makes it easier to interrupt a conversation already in progress. If you're braving the event on your own, I can totally relate and have some tips to help:

- Go with a specific time frame in mind. You can say, "I'll stay for one hour, then leave," for example. When the time is up, head home without any guilt, and don't forget you can always employ the Irish goodbye!

- To approach a stranger, scan the room for someone or something to compliment. I always look for a fellow female with a cute bag or shoes. Starting a conversation with a genuine compliment creates instant rapport and disarms the other person quickly.

- Bring your own business cards, but always ask for the other person's card first. Do not hand out your card unless specifically asked for it. It comes off as presumptuous.

- Focus on connecting with only a few people, rather than trying to meet everyone in the room. Quality versus quantity. As you collect business cards, put them in separate pockets—one for people you want to follow up with and one for people you didn't click with and don't care to build a relationship with. That second pocketful can live on an email-only drip campaign or go straight into the trash, whichever you prefer.

- Ask those few people if they would like to have coffee or lunch, and tell them you'll follow up tomorrow with them to set a date.

- Follow up tomorrow and set a date!

- Relax and have fun.

Following up is just as important as attending the event, if not more so. Be sure to follow up right away and create a plan to stay in touch. I always follow up with a handwritten "nice meeting you" note, as long as I can find an address. As we learned in an earlier chapter, handwritten notes are memorable and unique, and people appreciate the extra effort and personal touch!

Networking events are fantastic ways to meet people. It's important for us introverts to embrace them our own way, which means monitoring our energy during and after the event, allowing ourselves the permission to leave when we need to leave, and not planning too many events too close together. There was a time early in my career when I was out at an event four to five nights a week. It was exhausting, and it wasn't sustainable. Find your balance and stick to it. If it's twice a month, great! If it's twice a week, great! Again, trial and error will help you hone in on the sweet spot for you.

Thirty-Three

Get Out of Your Comfort Zone (But Only for Ten Minutes)

How many times have we all heard we need to get out of our comfort zones to be successful? More than you can count? Same here. I understand and agree with the principle, but I take issue with gurus neglecting to give more context to the theory. It's absolutely true that in order to build a business, be successful, or really to do anything worth doing in life, there's an aspect that requires stepping outside of your comfort zone.

However, it's not helpful to say, "Hey, go outside your comfort zone," and leave it at that. It's actually borderline irresponsible. The implication is you need to stay outside your comfort zone for long periods of time (or forever, depending on your guru of choice). That's just not true. It's not healthy, normal, or achievable. It's also not necessary.

You only need to step out of your comfort zone for ten minutes or less to do the important, scary thing. Usually, it's lead generation or the beginning of your lead gen activity. It's walking in the door to the event and starting the first conversation. After that initial discomfort, most of us will feel more at ease. We'll settle into the event, grab a coffee or a glass of wine, start talking to someone, and be perfectly fine.

No one can live outside their comfort zone. Don't try. And don't beat yourself up when you can't do it. No one can. This is why it's so critically important to be strategic in your lead gen activities, to focus your time and energy on what will have the biggest impact in your business. During the first year or two of any agent's career, the game is to find the tactics that work for them as quickly and efficiently as possible. Once you know what works for you, you'll be able to allocate the appropriate amount of resources to those lead gen strategies. With time and consistency, not only will you see more results, you'll become more comfortable. The stress and mental energy required will decrease significantly. It does get easier. I promise.

Years ago, I was a founding member of a new BNI chapter. This is the largest international networking organization in the world, with (usually) only one real estate agent per chapter. Fun fact: Ivan Misner, the founder of BNI, is a fellow introvert! Our chapter met weekly at 7 a.m. and passed referrals to one another. During every meeting, each of us would stand up and give a sixty-second pitch. We grew to about fifty members, so every week, I'd stand up in front of the group and speak. It was nerve-wracking every single time, but each week, I grew more comfortable. The level of dreading my turn decreased. It never went away, but spending sixty seconds outside of my comfort zone once per week resulted in long-lasting friendships, improved public speaking skills, and real estate referrals. A little bit of discomfort was well worth it. And I always felt better knowing it was temporary. My pitch was always over before I knew it.

Thirty-Four

Relationship-Building

All business is based on relationships. People work with people they know, they like, they trust, and they *remember*. The goal is to have enough people in our network who know, like, trust, and remember us. That last one is key. Many agents master the first three. They know a lot of people, are very personable, build trust with their networks, yet they fail to generate as much repeat and referral business as they could because they lack the systems to stay in touch regularly.

Have you ever been scrolling on social media and come across a past client's post saying they just moved? You had sold them their house a few years ago. You thought you'd kept in touch. You sent a nice closing gift, followed by a holiday card each year. You hit "Like" on their Facebook posts sometimes, when you happen to see them. How dare they sell and buy with someone else?

We have all been there. It's a punch to the gut initially, but we only have ourselves to blame. It is not the consumer's job to remember us. They're busy. They're self-absorbed (we all are). They don't care. Our job is to stay top of mind with them, so when the time comes for someone to move, they call us. Another term for this is emotional proximity.

You can achieve this by providing exceptional customer service to your current clients, staying in constant communication with them after the transaction, and making it easy for them to refer you to their friends and family. The communication part is what more agents struggle with. Don't worry—you do not have to call everyone in your database every month, but multiple means of communication over the course of a year is key. In the section on Follow Up in Section 4, we will go over the entire touch system in detail. This is your guide for keeping in touch and building relationships. It's a combination of multiple touch points throughout the year, rather than calling the same people every single month. This way, everyone in your network is hearing from you many times throughout the year, but because the mediums are varied, it will feel like consistency without being too salesy.

Provide value in every communication as well. Market statistics and home maintenance tips are easy to pull together and interesting to most people. An invitation to an event is an amazing touch, as it's a show of appreciation. Updates on your career are good to include to mix it up, but I wouldn't recommend leaning too heavily on those.

Thirty-Five

Entrepreneurs' Guilt

I'm writing this chapter on a Sunday afternoon. It's rainy and a bit chilly outside. I'm sitting at a restaurant's bar, enjoying alfredo pasta with chicken and broccoli. Thankfully, I'm a regular here, so they don't mind me having my laptop open on the bar. Once I'm done with this chapter, I'm heading home to take a nap. Years ago, I would have felt incredibly guilty about taking a nap during the day, even on a weekend. It's a common phenomenon I call Entrepreneurs' Guilt.

The feeling that "I should be working" and "I should be doing more" is pervasive in our industry. It stems from a lack of boundaries and is exacerbated when there's a lack of sales. It's common and normal, yet this flavor of negative self-talk is counterproductive. It is difficult to pull yourself out of the guilt loop once you're in it, and it's nearly impossible to enjoy a relaxing activity while simultaneously feeling guilty about taking the time to do it.

What's a better use of time and energy: taking a well-deserved hour-long nap after a productive morning of lead generation and lead follow up or wrestling with "should I or shouldn't I?" and wasting over an hour in these mental deliberations? Worse, if you then decide to take the nap, chances are you won't be able to sleep anyway and will wake up feeling even more guilty.

So what's the solution? Release the guilt. Naps are just one example of activities we feel guilty about doing, but this could apply to anything. Release the "I should" or "I should not" self-talk. I realize this is easier said than done. The first step is to catch yourself saying it. The next time you use the word "should" with yourself, notice it. Become aware of it. Then reframe it by replacing the word with "choose." For instance: "I should not take a nap because I should be working more instead" becomes "I choose to take a nap strategically after completing my goals today" or "I choose to take a nap so I can bring my best energy to the networking event I'm attending this evening."

Everything is a choice. Assigning shame or guilt to these choices isn't helpful. This will get easier with practice and with increased confidence in your choices. Of course, if you're napping all day long and not doing what needs to be done in your business, that's the only time the guilty feeling is trying to tell you something worthwhile. So keep balance in mind, but also be aware of how drained you feel after your lead gen activities (refer back to chapter 4). If something isn't working or is sucking the life out of you, make a different choice.

Thirty-Six

Social Media

While social media is no longer a new concept, for some real estate agents, it still feels like a frontier in many ways. If you're someone to whom social media content-creation and marketing come naturally, and you enjoy it, keep at it! Do what works for you and what you enjoy.

If you do not fall into that category, stick with me. I have exciting news: You do not need to be on social media to have a successful business. I know there are people out there who disagree with me on this point, but social media is not a requirement, and it never will be. There are plenty of other ways to get your name out there and connect with new people. So if you are absolutely terrified of having a social media presence or feel strongly against it, that's okay. Your business will still grow; you simply will need to implement alternative strategies. Pick any others from this section on lead generation, and make it happen.

If you're somewhere in the middle, it's worth considering trying out social media marketing. Unless you're running ads, it doesn't cost any money, making it a great option for agents who are early in their careers or have a tighter budget for marketing. You're able to reach a lot of people—hundreds, thousands, or even millions—all from the comfort of your home or office. For this reason, social media is a fantastic tool for us introverts, especially when it comes to preserving our energy.

A potential downside is the perceived requirement to put yourself out there, sharing about your personal life online. But that's not necessary. Here are some ideas for social media content that are not too personal yet enable your audience to feel connected to you (remember—emotional proximity):

- Interview local business owners, such as cafe owners, hair stylists, or even your go-to mechanic. This is also a great way to cross-promote and reach a wider audience.

- Post about your favorite local hot spots or hidden gems in your town.

- Tell your clients' success stories after each transaction (keeping personal details private/anonymous, of course).

- Post photos of your pet (this is my favorite strategy. At this point, most of my followers know and love my cat).

- Share something delicious you cooked for dinner.

- Write a quick review of a book you recently read (YES, you can absolutely post about how helpful this book is and encourage your followers to buy a copy! Thanks for asking).

- Ask a question. Questions are beneficial for boosting engagement on social media platforms. Example: "Real estate through the years"—ask your followers to guess the average price for a home in your town in different years. What did a home cost in 2005? How about in 1997? Or 1982?

- Talk about the market, but keep it interesting and easy for the general public to understand. Example: How many homes are currently for sale in your town? What's the average price? How many more homes are available now versus a year ago? Steer clear of industry jargon like absorption rates and so on. People might not understand it, and they will lose interest.

The key to using social media as a lead generation strategy is to choose one or two platforms and master them. This includes posting your own content consistently, as well as interacting with your followers' content consistently. Time-block thirty minutes per day to react/like and comment on other peoples' posts/stories, and time-block to create your own content. You do not need to post something everyday to start having an impact, but I'd post something at least once per week.

When choosing which platform(s) to use, think about where you're most likely to find your ideal audience and what type of content you want to create. The Facebook crowd is very different from the TikTok crowd. YouTube is the best option (currently) for creating longer videos, while Instagram is a good place for shorter videos (stories). Who do you want to reach, where are they spending most of their time online, and what's your preferred type of content to create consistently? Do some research online and decide what makes the most sense for your business.

Thirty-Seven
Create Your Lead Gen Plan

Okay, great, so you have lots of lead gen ideas—some are probably familiar to you, and perhaps several are new to you. The tactics we've covered are just a few of the many possible strategies you can use to find new business. I recommend choosing just three to five strategies to implement at one time.

How do you start putting your plan together, though? This is where most agents get stuck. By stuck, I mean they have a notebook full of incredible ideas they take zero action on. I know. I've done this many, many times over the years. It's easy to learn about a new strategy and get excited, but that won't get you more business. Only action will. Putting together a lead generation plan and finding the accountability to take action on it are what my clients who hire me for 1:1 coaching typically need the most help with. While I'd love to coach everyone who reads this book, I'd also like to give you the answers so you can tackle this on your own.

Here are the steps to creating your own custom lead gen plan:

1. **Start with an audit.** It's important to take a look back on what you've tried before. Make a list of every single lead gen strategy you've employed in the past. If you're brand new to real estate, go ahead and skip to step five.

2. **Go through your list and rank how effective each strategy has been from one to ten.** One means it didn't work at all. Ten means it generated multiple pieces of closed business.

3. **Go through your list a second time and rank how much you enjoyed each strategy from one to ten.** One means you absolutely hate this activity. You dread it and would be thrilled to never do it again. Ten means you love it, enjoy it, and look forward to it each and every time.

4. **Make some strategic choices.** Include anything in your lead gen strategy that falls above a seven on both the effectiveness scale and the enjoyment scale. Get rid of anything below a three on both scales (without feeling any guilt). Those strategies in the middle can be kept, deleted, or delegated to someone else. If any strategy is extremely effective yet not at all enjoyable, that would be a good one to delegate or leverage. Pay someone else to do it, so you don't have to!

5. **Add to your list to create your lead gen plan (or start your list from scratch, if you're a new agent).** Use the strategies in the previous chapters as a starting point. Pri-

oritize the ones that feel exciting to you, and avoid any that sound terrible.

6. **Balance your lead gen plan.** Ideally, you want a combination of free (social media posts and comments) and paid (client appreciation events), as well as time-intensive (cold calling), and highly-leveraged (automated emails that go out to your database monthly). Stick to no more than five strategies at once; otherwise, you'll spread yourself too thin, and none of your tactics will receive the effort required to produce the desired results.

7. **Translate your lead gen plan into your calendar.** Now that you have your list of strategies, make sure they all live in your calendar consistently. Sending one postcard to your neighborhood is not a strategy, but sending one postcard every month for a year is a great way to farm your neighborhood, for example. Go back to the chapter on time blocking if you need a refresher on this topic.

8. **Stick with it.** Congrats! You have your plan in place, and it's grounded in your calendar to make sure everything actually gets done. Do not give up. Decide how long you'll work each strategy to give it a fair shot, then do the work and don't stop. An accountability partner will be extremely helpful for this. Partner up with another agent in your office, hire a coach, or join a community of like-minded agents. For a free online community, join our Facebook group called "Introverts in Real Estate."

9. **Track your results.** Don't forget this part! Tracking will make your life much easier the next time you audit your lead gen strategy—this should be done at least once per year if not quarterly. Track how much money you spend on each strategy, how much time you spend, how much energy it takes, and how much business you've found. Include all leads and referrals in addition to active and closed clients. A simple Google Sheet or Excel is the perfect tool for this type of tracking.

Take Action:

- Audit your previous and current lead generation activities. List them and rate each one's results one to ten, then rate each one's joy factor one to ten (how much you enjoy the activity).

- Make your decisions about which activities to keep, which to delete, which to delegate, and which to add—this is the foundation for your lead gen plan!

- Find other successful agents who have done every activity you haven't tried before, and borrow their system. Always feel free to use our Facebook group, "Introverts in Real Estate," as a place to ask for advice and find others who've done what you are looking to do.

- Remind yourself daily that your job is to go find people in the world who need or want to buy or sell real estate. Set a daily reminder in your phone, or use sticky notes until this habit is built and your mindset is shifted for good.

Part IV

Working With Clients (Without Burning Out)

Finesse Literary Press Ltd.

"The reason so many small businesses fail, however, is because passion alone can't cut it. For passion to survive, it needs structure. A WHY without the HOWs, passion without structure, has a very high probability of failure."

Simon Sinek, Start With Why

Thirty-Eight
Working With Sellers

There's a reason why Gary Keller stresses the 3Ls: leads, listings, and leverage in *The Millionaire Real Estate Agent*. Working with sellers is typically less time-consuming than running around with buyers, making offer after offer, getting outbid, and worrying that the buyers may just decide to give up and rent for another year.

The listing side of the real estate business is also more rooted in data. It involves pricing at a high level, strategic marketing, and expert negotiation. For us introverts, it's easier to plan our energy output with sellers, as most seller appointments are set in advance. You can plan for them. You have more control of the transaction's timing as well. You choose (along with the sellers) when the open houses will be, how showings will be handled, and when the offer deadlines are. No wonder I personally decided to focus on working exclusively with sellers when I stepped back into sales.

Many agents stress about the listing appointment (understandably), so I'd like to share my own listing appointment strategy with you. It's very simple: Ask a lot of questions, show enthusiasm, and be overly prepared.

Ask questions, listen to the answers, acknowledge what they said, then ask more questions. Rather than worrying about giving the perfect "listing presentation" that showcases your skills and experience, make the entire appointment about the sellers and their goals. After all, it's about serving the client. Here are my favorite questions to ask (feel free to adjust the words a bit to fit your own voice, but avoid beginning a question with the word "why," as it seems accusatory):

- So tell me about your plans! OR So you're thinking about moving? (Ask as many follow up questions as you can to get to their ultimate root motivation).

- What about that is important to you? OR What will that do for you and your family?

- Where are you headed?

- What do you love about your home?

- What improvements or updates have you made since you bought it?

- When would you like to close, ideally?

- What price do you have in mind?

- What's most important to you in the agent you choose? (Only ask this if you know they are interviewing other agents).

- Is there anything you were hoping we'd cover today that we haven't yet discussed? (Ask this towards the end of the meeting).

- Which service package would you like? (Use this if you have a tiered commission structure, which is a great strategy I use, as it gives sellers a choice and helps them feel ownership of the decision. In a highly-educated area like Boston, this is even more important).

Show enthusiasm. During my first year in real estate, I cold-called hundreds of expired listings. I sat through a class where I was taught that cold calling was the best/only way to build a business from scratch, so that's what I did. It was painful, but I did it. I went on many appointments and became the definition of "failing forward." I will never forget one seller I cold-called and had a listing appointment with. She ultimately decided not to hire me because I was not enthusiastic enough about her house during the appointment; I thought I had been, but her perception was very different from mine.

I learned this valuable lesson only because I asked her what influenced her decision after she told me she was hiring someone else—so always ask, even if you're afraid to hear the answer! I never made that mistake again. Being enthusiastic and excited takes more energy than normal, and it's a conscious effort to make my energy level match or exceed that of my prospective client. Fake it a bit if you need to. The listing appointment is the only time I will ever tell you it's okay to fake it!

Be overly prepared. Do your homework and come as prepared as you possibly can. Most sellers won't need to review everything you prepared, but when you meet that engineer type, they will be impressed by your knowledge. Here's a quick list of what you should prepare ahead of every listing appointment:

- Market data for the specific town/city: average days on market, current inventory, average list price to sale price percentage.

- Comps: recently sold properties (of course), pendings, actives, as well as any expired, canceled, or withdrawn properties. This will give you a comprehensive picture of the market activity for properties like the subject property you're hopefully going to sell.

- Online valuations: While we know the real estate portals are based on algorithms and aren't accurate, it's important to know what the seller sees their property valued at. Check all the major real estate websites for a full view.

- Your own stats: Don't make this the focus of the meeting, but it's good to have this information just in case the seller asks. How many homes have you sold in the area? What's your average list price to sale price?

Be sure you're well-rested before every listing appointment. Make these appointments your top priority in your calendar, at least in terms of real estate activities. I prefer to stick to one listing appointment per day maximum. This way, I can be sure to bring my very best energy to the sellers each time. Give yourself permission to reschedule other things if you need to conserve your energy or even schedule in a nap beforehand. Respect your needs and take care of yourself. This will give you the best chance of winning the listing.

Thirty-Nine

Working With Buyers

Some agents absolutely love working with buyers. For certain personality types (if you're familiar with the DISC assessment, the high I and high S personalities) are well-suited to helping buyers. In general, there's much more time spent on a buyer client than on a listing. There are also more conversations, which not only require more time but also a lot more energy. When working with buyers, we introverts have to be careful not to expend too much of our energy without properly managing it.

Showings are the best example. A full day of buyer showings is taxing for any real estate agent, but it's especially draining for introverts. During every showing, you have to be "on"—happy, energetic, ready to answer hundreds of questions, trying not to get lost driving from house to house, stressing about the buyers getting lost driving from house to house, keeping the buyers' children calm yet entertained, prying open frozen lockboxes, turning off and on every light in every property...are you exhausted just reading this? I am!

No, I am not aiming to convince you not to work with buyers. I am, however, acknowledging the intensity of the energy drain that can happen when working with buyers if you aren't carefully managing your energy. How? Here's my advice for setting expectations very early on in your work with a new buyers—have these conversations at your initial buyer consult, and your experience will be more effective and enjoyable:

- Talk about the ideal showings schedule. I always tell buyers I recommend looking at no more than four homes in one day. This is for their own sanity and mine and to prevent them from getting confused. There will be situations when buyers are flying in from out of state for one weekend, and you need to pack the schedule, but this should be the exception, not the rule.

- Let buyers know most sellers require at least twenty-four hours' notice to set up a private showing. Humanize the sellers by telling buyers that the sellers need some notice to pack up their kids and pets, get them out of the house, and clean up as much as possible to make a good impression on the buyers. Every private showing also requires coordinating the sellers' schedule, the listing agent's schedule (when accompanied), and your schedule as the agent. A lot of moving parts need to come together for each and every showing. It's good to tell the buyers this, so they understand and appreciate the work that's involved.

- Encourage buyers to attend open houses without you. If you're available and want to go with them, that's totally fine, but if you know they will want to see dozens of houses before making an offer, open houses are great leverage for you. Let the buyers know that if they find something they love and want to make an offer, you'll go see the house for yourself ASAP. You can even give them a stack of your business cards to bring to open houses, so they can attempt to avoid signing in.

- Share with your buyer clients the average number of homes your buyers typically view before making an offer. By educating buyers about the process, you'll adjust their expectations about how many properties you're going to show them. Here's what it sounds like: "I'll send you every available home that meets your criteria via email. Then I'd recommend you take some time and drive by the homes you think you'll like to check out the area, the street, and the yard. At that point, let me know which homes you'd like to schedule a private showing for if there's no open house. This way, we'll narrow it down and focus on the homes most likely to be the right fit for you. Think of it as a process of elimination to find your ideal home. For reference, most of my buyers tour five properties before making their first offer—that's the average."

Notice in that last paragraph, I said "making their *first* offer" rather than "making an offer." Another vital part of working with buyers is helping them understand the current market. Perhaps you're reading this book in a part of the country where you're in a buyers' market. In most of the greater Boston area, we are still in a strong sellers' market. Either way, let the buyers know what to expect. This is your opportunity to provide incredible value by educating them and being the local expert. Interpreting the hyper-local market data and communicating it helpfully to buyers is one of the advantages of working with a real estate professional, and as we know, more and more buyers seem to think they do not need an agent. Help them see why they need you.

One way you can prepare and educate your buyers is: Ask yourself if they will need to avoid looking at new listings when they first come on the market because there will be many other offers or if the buyers in your market have the upper hand. Consider the specific areas and types of properties they're looking for and the price point, as local markets can vary greatly even within the same city. As I write this, any single family home under one million dollars in my market is considered an entry level-priced listing and is selling hundreds of thousands above asking, while there are dozens of ultra-luxury new construction properties that have been sitting for months.

Bring your buyers a sampling of actively for sale, pending, and sold properties to help educate them about how far their budget will get them. Do they need to prepare themselves for being outbid multiple times? If you're in a sellers' market and your buyer insists on getting a "deal," you'll know what kinds of properties you'll be limited to: anything that's been sitting on the market for at least two weeks, For Sale By Owner listings, and off-market properties. The more you prepare your buyers for what to expect in the market and how the process works, the better experience you'll all have. It's leverage for you and your energy, and it's also providing a high level of customer service. Win-win!

Forty

Open Houses

(Part 2)

Take a nap after you host your open houses. That is all.

Forty-One

Managing Communication

One of the best tools for managing your time and energy is managing your communication. This applies to communication with your clients, your vendors, and the agents on the opposite side of the transactions. How many times have you heard real estate agents say they're available twenty-four hours a day, seven days a week? Whenever I hear this from a new agent, I quickly jump in to educate them. When I hear this from a top agent who's influencing others from a position of authority, I cringe.

I am not a real estate robot, and neither are you. We are humans. We need to eat, sleep, drink water, exercise, and take care of our physical and mental health in order to survive and function at a high level. Humans are not meant to be available for phone calls and texts at all times. It's not normal, natural, or healthy. Yet real estate agents run around bragging about our availability. We do it to ourselves.

In absence of any other value (or perhaps due to simply a lack of confidence communicating any other value), we extol the virtue of unlimited availability. The reality is this cheapens us.

Being "always available" actually lessens our clients' perception of our professionalism and value. Think about it this way: If you need to hire the best defense attorney money can buy, would you want the one who answers her own phone and responses to your texts at midnight or the one who requires setting up a meeting in advance because her time is so valuable? Another example: getting a haircut. I only get haircuts once or twice each year, and because I've moved around the country a few times, I don't have a go-to salon. So I do my research online, read reviews, and ask for recommendations. You'll never find me in a salon that accepts walk-ins. This is the perception of value. I could be totally wrong, and the walk-in salon down the street could be the best one around, but I don't perceive it that way.

Of course, we can't be quite as strict as an in-demand lawyer or a top hair salon in a major city. Having a three month waitlist isn't realistic for most real estate agents nor is it practical. The point is that we control how our clients, leads, and the public perceive us, and one of the ways we can actively control that is through our communication. Here are some strategies for managing your communication:

- Set your working hours. In Part 2, we touched on the concept of setting working hours when we discussed setting boundaries with clients. It's easy enough to communicate what your hours are, yet it can be challenging to stick to them, especially if you've been in the industry for years and have not built the habit of maintaining communication boundaries. You can tell clients you are available from 9 a.m. to 6 p.m.

unless there's an emergency (adjust the times according to what works best for you). Most people will understand and respect you more for respecting your own time.

- Always remain calm on the outside, even when you're freaking out on the inside. Negotiating and delivering any less-than-stellar news should always be done over the phone. You're likely to find yourself in situations where you're on the phone with someone who's unhappy, maybe even angry. Your job is always to remain calm. Express empathy for the other person, understand their point of view, but don't let your emotions take over. This is a skill that takes a lot of practice for some personality types, and it's worth investing the time to hone it. One note on negotiating: check out the book *Never Split the Difference* by Chris Voss for exceptional negotiation tactics involving communication.

- Schedule calls ahead of time whenever possible. Even if it's later the same day, scheduling a call with a client gives you some lead time to prepare and get to the best possible location. As introverts, we tend to perform better when we are prepared, calm, and in a quiet environment that's conducive to critical thinking. The office is my favorite place to take calls, but I do take a lot of calls in my car when I'm on the road. Knowing when most of my calls will be in advance allows me to plan around them and not sound flustered on the phone.

- Take communication breaks. If you're talking to people all day long, it's inevitable to feel drained afterward. That's one of the definitions of being an introvert! So give yourself permission to take breaks. Sometimes, the most accessible and convenient quiet place is the car, and that's okay. Let yourself have ten minutes (or more) of uninterrupted silence. It's not a waste of time; it's a necessary recharge of your energy.

For more on communication with clients, I'd recommend checking out the book *Fierce Conversations* by Susan Scott.

Forty-Two
Home Inspections and Closings

When I was a solo agent, working with both buyers and sellers, home inspections felt like running a marathon. In Massachusetts, inspections run anywhere from two to four hours, which means a lot of time standing around a house listening to the inspector and making polite small talk with your buyers (and sometimes their parents). Closings are similar, although the mood is happier because we're at the finish line. Lots of small talk, lots of listening. Yes, it is completely normal to feel drained after these parts of the transaction.

That's totally okay. Just plan for it! Know you might be drained afterwards and don't schedule a multi-million dollar listing appointment right after an inspection or a closing. Have the appointment first. By the way, this is another reason I prefer working with sellers. I realize norms vary throughout the country, and in my area, listing agents rarely go to their closings. If they do attend the home inspection, it's usually just at the end to ensure everything went well. As you can tell, it all comes down to energy management and being strategic with your scheduling.

Forty-Three

Follow Up

Follow up until they "buy or die." Isn't that the saying? It's crass, but it's true. Persistent follow-up is the most underutilized activity in building a successful real estate business. Many agents I coach and train think it's all about lead generation. It's not. Lead follow up is more impactful and vital than lead generation. Think about it: You already went through all the work to find the lead, and chances are, most leads are not ready to buy or sell real estate the day you first meet them. Putting systems in place to make sure every lead is followed up with regularly and consistently is key.

Some leads will be ready within a few weeks or a month of meeting them while others won't be ready for years. The longer your prospective client's timeline, the more critical your follow-up is. We cannot expect people to remember us after years of not staying in touch. It's our job to keep in touch, stay top of mind, and provide value, so when the time is right for the individual client, they'll know who to call. Make it easy for them.

An agent I used to work with had an open house lead she followed up with multiple times throughout the year for two years straight with no response. Picture that: You meet a buyer at an open house, reach out to them to follow up, and they don't answer the phone or respond to your text. Most agents will try one more time (maybe) then give up. This agent persisted. She called or texted this buyer every few months for two full years, and they never responded to her. It was radio silence until the day they were finally ready to buy. Then they called her. She not only had stayed top of mind but had proven her tenacity as an agent by not giving up on them. If that's not a compelling story to show you the value of following up, I don't know what is!

I am usually asked: How often do I follow up? What medium should I use to follow up (call/text/email)? And what do I say? The answers are tied together. I subscribe to the traditional thirty-three-touch method or some variation of it. The thirty-three-touch is thirty-three communication points to each lead over the course of a year. It sounds like a lot, but when you vary the mediums and lead with valuable content/communication, it doesn't feel like too much. The basic breakdown is: a monthly email, a monthly postcard in the mail, four calls or texts per year, two in-person meetings (can be 1:1 or hanging out at your client events), plus an end of the year gift that the lead will see multiple times, like a calendar or a sports schedule magnet.

You can tweak the frequency and the mediums to match your goals and your brand. For instance, feel free to swap out calls for social media direct messages for some leads if that's how you have already communicated with them. If anyone would think it's strange for you to be calling them, skip the call and text or DM instead. This will make your leads feel more comfortable with you since you're communicating with them in the style they prefer.

The bottom line is to persistently communicate with every lead multiple times in multiple ways until they tell you to stop or they become a client. Do not give up. This is tough for everyone, but it can be especially tricky for us introverts. We don't want to feel like we're bothering people. That's a very real concern and a valid feeling. The solution? Add value, keep it interesting, and entertain them.

There's a reason why there are an abundance of real estate reality shows on the air. People are fascinated and entertained by real estate! You can use this to your advantage. While market stats and information about interest rates have their place and do fall under the category of adding value, I would limit that content to a few times a year and focus the bulk of your communication on properties themselves. Houses. That's what people want to see. Give the people what they want. Make it entertaining while also educating your leads.

Example: Post a photo and brief stats about a listing (yours or someone else's, with their permission) and invite your followers to guess the price. This is an easy way to engage your audience, entertain them, and educate them when you eventually tell them the price. You can use this strategy with just sold listings, with active listings, or even with coming soon listings that aren't even on the market yet. That third option prevents people from looking it up on Zillow and cheating.

Find creative ways to keep in touch and follow up that are interesting and valuable to the person you're communicating with. Before you send out any texts, make any calls, blast any emails, or post on social media, ask yourself: How would I react if I received this? Is it worth receiving? What would I think about the person who sent it? Is it self-serving? Then decide what to tweak before sending. Don't give up, even if they don't respond. People are busy. Be careful not to take it personally or be offended when people don't get back to you. Notice I said "when" not "if." The majority of people will not reply to you. That's ok. Keep following up, then follow up some more.

Forty-Four
Working With Vendors

You may think you don't have a team if you're a solo real estate agent. But you do. Your vendors are your team. Mortgage lenders, real estate attorneys/title companies, homeowners' insurance companies, home inspectors, handymen, photographers/videographers, and stagers comprise your team of professionals that could make or break your transactions. At the very least, they could determine how seamlessly each deal goes. A bad vendor can blow up a deal. A great vendor can save deals. I've experienced both.

Take the time and effort to curate your list of preferred vendors. You'll hire some directly, so you'll have complete control over who you use—for instance, the photographer you hire to take amazing photos of your listings is hired and paid by you. The sellers are not involved in the vetting or hiring process of this vendor. The lender, on the other hand, is chosen by the buyer. Period. However, you can make suggestions and explain to your buyers the benefits of working with a lender you have a good relationship with.

One of the most significant benefits in working with a lender you know and trust is ease of communication and availability when something goes wrong in the transaction. I like to tell buyers I prefer working with local lenders (versus a huge national company that requires dialing a 1-800 number) because if there's a problem, I can drive down to their office and kick their butt in person. This gets a laugh every time because I'm little and the exact opposite of intimidating, but it gets my point across in a memorable way because it's so unexpected. It also gives me an opportunity to showcase my passion for fighting for my clients before they even hire me. Whenever I explained this to a potential buyer client (usually sitting across the table at a Panera), I intentionally increased my excitement and energy to show them that there was some fire in me, and I'd use it when needed. So it served as an additional conversion tool during my buyer consultations.

Another benefit of encouraging your buyers to work with a local lender you've worked with before is it makes their offer more attractive. On the listing side, I always call the lenders on every pre-approval I receive. If the buyer's agent can tell me they've worked with the lender before, it strengthens the buyer's offer. It's even better when I have personally worked with the bank or mortgage broker before. I know my file will get extra special attention because of the relationship. This is a relationship business, and the vendor list is no exception.

We introverts tend to people-please while also trying to protect our energy. If I had lunch with every single mortgage broker who reached out to me, I would be exhausted (I also wouldn't have any time to sell houses). So it's important to pick and choose. Use your energy and time wisely and limit vendor meetings to once or twice a week at most. There's a friendly way to decline an offer of lunch or coffee if too many are coming in at once. Here's what to say: "I would love to meet with you! I don't have the bandwidth right now, but could you check in with me in a few months?" We talked about this in the section about Saying No, yet it's worth repeating here.

I always advise agents to have three or four different vendors in each category, in case your top person has an emergency and isn't available or they aren't a good match for a particular client. Build a deep bench of vendors. This will make you a better real estate agent, providing more value to your clients, even if they're not aware of it.

One last note on building your vendor relationships. Do business with people you like. Yes, they need to be great at what they do, but excellence is not hard to find. If there are twenty incredible real estate attorneys in your local area, why not choose to do business with the three or four you click with on a personal level? It will make things even more enjoyable for you. Some may think it's unprofessional, but I think it's wonderful to become friends with my vendors when possible. If you can find vendors who are also introverts or are introvert-friendly and appreciate your need for alone time, even better.

Forty-Five

Hiring Talent

Maybe you're already at the point in your career where you're thinking about or are in the process of hiring someone. This could be an admin, a showing assistant, an ISA, or another role on your team. Maybe you're far past that, and you already run a large team. Maybe you're not even close to that and just getting started building your business.

Years ago, I was at a place in my career where I contemplated hiring someone and starting a team. I was in the top twenty percent of my office and was making a decent living. My coach was encouraging me to build a team since that's what most agents did when they hit my level of success. Yet I resisted. Something held me back. I wasn't entirely able to articulate it then, but I certainly can now. I did not want to be responsible for someone else's livelihood. The thought of that terrified me. It seemed like an enormous amount of pressure, and frankly, it didn't seem worth the energy required to build it, manage it, and grow it.

Choosing not to build a team is one of the potential mistakes I've made in my career. I say potential because no one can predict an outcome with any amount of certainty. It could have been incredible. It could have been an absolute disaster. But the choice I made was mine, and I stand by it. Rather than building a team, I started a coaching company, something that was one hundred percent mine and completely within my control. I had no employees to train, no payroll to lose sleep over, and no pressure to perform to sustain another full-time role.

I do not share this story to scare you. I share it to empower you to make the right choice for your business. In certain circles, there's a well-worn path to success, and for some agents, that path can seem like the only option. But that's simply not true. I've always found it ironic that on one hand, we're told to build a life by design, and on the other, we're told to follow those who came before you and do exactly what they did. Your business is yours to create and grow however you desire. Break the mold. Follow your gut. Don't be afraid, and do not apologize for your choices.

My path eventually led me to full-time coaching, speaking on stages in front of thousands of people, and becoming a paid contributing writer to a leading industry magazine. It then led me to joining one of the top real estate teams in the country and creating a one-of-a-kind role within that organization. Guess how many people I'm responsible for. One—me. My stress level has never been lower. It's taken years of trial and error to get here, and yes, it was worth it.

For you, perhaps building or growing your team is the right path. For many agents, it is. And there's a reason for it. A team can be the best way to leverage your time and energy with the right people at the right time in the right roles. When the stars align, teams are fantastic.

How do you know when you're ready to make your first hire? Despite what some of the gurus will say, the answer is simple: when you have too many leads or not enough time. When you have too many leads, you need help to follow up, convert, and service all of them. This could be in the form of a talented executive assistant or a buyer's agent. When you don't have enough time, a virtual assistant or transaction coordinator should be your first hire. They're a perfect first hire because they are usually either part-time or paid per transaction. This minimizes your risk.

While I never built a team, I did hire a TC for a few years. For four hundred dollars per transaction, she handled all the paperwork and even communicated with my clients on my behalf to coordinate logistics and keep them up to date. It was the best money I'd ever spent. If you're thinking about hiring a TC, write down how many hours you spend on each transaction on average. Then find out how much a TC costs—it may have increased since I hired mine. Do the math. Is it worth it? For many agents, it is.

Let's say you're ready to hire your first or your tenth agent. This can get tricky. The natural inclination for most people is to hire other agents who are similar to them in personality and style. I'd say that's a mistake, usually. If your goal is to create a well-rounded team, hire people who are unique but you still get along with. . Keep in mind that skills can be taught. Attitude cannot. One of my favorite hiring hacks is to create a somewhat convoluted hiring process, like requiring applicants to include a specific predetermined phrase in their email subject line to prove that they pay attention to detail. Full disclosure:

I heard about this strategy while listening to the Empire Building podcast (check it out).

Know that hiring will be an energy-suck. It could very well be worth it, and I know that no one really talks about the negatives to hiring, so I felt it important to include it here. Hiring will be taxing, and when you do hire someone, training and managing them will also be an incredible energy-suck. People's lives change, their priorities change, and their motivation and attitude can change. Expect that going in. Have a plan in place to deal with it. That will save you a ton of headaches.

Take Action:

- Practice your listing and buyer consultations with peers in your office. The more you practice, the more confident you'll become, and your conversion rates will increase.

- Decide if there are any pieces of the transaction that are worth leveraging. Is there anything you absolutely hate doing? Consider hiring someone else to do it; this will conserve your energy in a big way.

- Determine your working hours, and decide if/how you'll communicate them to new clients.

Part V

Be a Proud Introvert Out in the World

Finesse Literary Press Ltd.

"Even if you're stretching yourself in the service of a core personal project, you don't want to act out of character too much or for too long...start by creating as many 'restorative niches' as possible in your daily life...a term for the place you go when you want to return to your true self. It can be a physical place, like the path beside the Richelieu River, or a temporal one, like the quiet breaks you plan between sales calls. It can mean canceling your social plans on the weekend before a big meeting at work, practicing yoga or meditation, or choosing e-mail over an in-person meeting."

Susan Cain, Quiet

Forty-Six

Should you tell people you're an introvert?

As much as being an introvert is part of our personalities, it's a much more individual trait than other parts of our personality. Lots of real estate training focuses on learning how to identify the personality of your prospect efficiently and effectively. I briefly mentioned the DISC assessment, which is a tried and true personality test that's extremely helpful in identifying quickly who's across the table from you. This tool is useful for determining how to approach the conversation: direct and to the point, story-telling and rapport-building, or highly detailed and comprehensive. Yet introversion is different. It's more internal. It has to do with your individual energy patterns rather than figuring out how your prospective client operates.

I am often asked how to determine whether your client/lead/prospect is an introvert or extrovert. The answer is simple but unpopular. It doesn't matter. It truly does not matter. And equally but oppositely, you do not need to tell your business contacts that you're an introvert.

Permit me to go on a tiny rant for a moment. One irritating downside of being an introvert is reading those horrible articles about introversion and the lists of professions that are "best-suited" for us or make excuses for why we can't perform at the same level of our extroverted counterparts. It's BS. Introverts have all the qualities to be better at sales and better leaders than extroverts—listening, problem solving, critical thinking. For this reason, I do not find it necessary or relevant to share the fact that you're an introvert with anyone outside of your most intimate personal and business relationships. There is too much bias and misinformation out there, and frankly, it's not worth the energy it would take to explain introversion to everyone you encounter.

Whether you're an introvert or an extrovert affects you and your family directly, no one else. Leave it be with clients. But you do need to have the conversation with whomever you live with or work with.

Imagine coming home from a full day of client meetings, calls, and sitting in traffic. You're completely drained, at about ten percent energy battery. Your partner wants to go out. There's a party down the street. What do you do? If you haven't yet explained to your partner how your energy works, they may not understand. I see so many couples fight because of unmatched expectations like this, and it's completely avoidable.

Having the conversation with your partner can be scary or awkward. If they're a reader, direct them to read what I'm sure you can now see is one of my favorite books: *Quiet* by Susan Cain. If they're not a reader, go ahead and blame me. Direct the awkwardness to the author of this book. "Honey, I read this book by this agent named Ashley, and I realized I'm actually an introvert and need alone time to recharge my energy." For anyone who's totally unfamiliar with this concept, it sounds pretty crazy. Uninformed people have no idea how to process this concept. But there's an opportunity to educate in a loving, patient manner.

You do not need to tell anyone you're an introvert except your partner. If you live with someone or work closely with someone, it will help to let them know how your energy flows. But it won't affect how you work with clients and leads.

Forty-Seven

Attracting Your Ideal Clients

There's enough business out there for all of us, but how do you ensure you're attracting the clients you'll love working with? The easiest and most natural strategy is to be yourself. Be proud of your true self without trying to change who you are. Your ideal client will choose to work with you because your personality and vibe will resonate with them. People feel comfortable with people who are similar to them. As much as people try to fight this, it's true.

You can use this truth to your advantage. Remember I told you about the listing I lost because I wasn't enthusiastic enough? The moral of the story was to go into your appointments with extra energy and enthusiasm. Yet stay within your natural energy levels when maximizing your enthusiasm. Think of it this way: Tap into your energy supply without crossing the line into being too fake. If you go too hard and start acting inauthentic, people can tell, and you're likely to lose all credibility.

If you are naturally more reserved and calm, you'll attract clients who are also reserved and calm. They will appreciate the fact that you are like them, and they'll feel more comfortable working with an agent who can keep them calm when the transaction gets rocky.

If you're more outgoing and exuberant, you'll find clients who want to work with someone like that. So no matter what your personality and style, you'll find clients who match you. Lean into it. Don't fight it. It will make your lead generation efforts much more effective and make your transactions more enjoyable (usually).

Forty-Eight
The Proud, Confident Introvert

Over the past several years of coaching and teaching classes to thousands of introverted agents, one of the most common sentiments I hear is borderline apologetic. People make excuses for how they act or why they're reserved. There's a pervasive vibe of feeling "less than" our extroverted counterparts. There's no polite way to say this—we have to cut that s*** out.

Introverts are incredibly powerful and necessary to the world and in the real estate industry. People need us. People want to work with us because of who we are, not in spite of it. The more proud we are, the more confidence we exude, and the more quickly people will trust us. Own who you are. Be proud!

Erica Smentowski, a solo introverted agent based in Florida, says:

> "Confidence is not the same as introversion, but they can work with or against each other. If you have confidence in your expertise and experience in the topic and are an introvert, you can still muster what it takes to door knock and make those calls. However, if you do not have confidence, that would draw too much energy and may discourage you from doing a task, such as door knocking."
>
> Erica Smentowski

You may be thinking: "That's great, but how do I actually make myself proud and confident?" I have a suggestion: positive self-talk, daily. I know it sounds stupid, but it works. Another term for this is affirmations. Repeat positive things about yourself in the mirror when you're getting ready each morning, in the car on the way to your first appointment, or before going to bed. Your subconscious mind will start to believe what you tell it, even if your conscious mind is skeptical.

List your accomplishments. Seriously. Every single thing you've ever accomplished in your entire life should be included in this list. Grab your laptop (or legal pad and felt tip pen if you're old school like me) and write down everything. It helps to think about your life in buckets, and I always recommend starting from childhood.

Were you given any special accolades or awards as a kid? Win a spelling bee? I remember being elected one of two student council representatives from my third grade class, and I felt so proud! Graduating high school is an accomplishment. Graduating college is an accomplishment. Did you graduate with honors? Were you a leader in any groups in school or did you start your own group? Did you excel in sports? Play a musical instrument? Maybe you had a challenging childhood, and surviving it is an incredible accomplishment on its own.

Next, consider your business achievements as an adult. Think about promotions you've earned at work, sales you've made, businesses you've started, awards you've received, people you've helped. If you need inspiration, read through all of your past client reviews. I'd actually suggest storing those in one place, so you can go back and reference them when you're having a rough day.

Think about personal accomplishments, too—your friendships, family, relationships, pets. Where have you wanted to travel and made it happen? Maybe you've invented something or written your own book. Maybe your social media posts inspire people. How have you improved the world, even in small ways? Did you ever give a waiter an overly generous tip and make their day? Write it down on your list.

Before we wrap up this chapter, I want to acknowledge that building confidence is a process. It takes time, and it's natural for confidence to ebb and flow. Even the most secure, confident people out there still have days when they feel the imposter syndrome, when they question themselves and want to give up. That happens to me, and it is one-hundred percent normal to experience self-doubt. Please be careful not to put pressure on yourself to be confident every moment of every day because that's not realistic. Remember: We are human. We are not Tesla real estate robots (at least not yet). We have emotions. We struggle. And we are also resilient and will get back up to keep moving forward.

Forty-Nine

Talk it Out or Sit in Silence?

One of the key differences between introverts and extroverts is how we process new information and challenges we face. Us introverts tend to process internally. We sit in silence with information while extroverts usually need to talk things through. My favorite extrovert, Keith, is a perfect example. We are lucky to have an incredibly close and open relationship in which we talk about everything in our lives and our businesses. He also works in real estate, so we always have a lot to talk about. Whenever there's a challenge he's facing, he processes it and problem solves by walking and talking...and smoking cigarettes. I walk next to him and listen (not smoking). I can almost see his brain working while he talks.

On the other hand, I process and problem-solve in silence. Sometimes I walk by myself, sometimes I write in my journal, and sometimes I sit quietly. Noise hinders my thinking. Talking doesn't help me until I've found a possible solution and want feedback on it.

You probably can already identify which end of the spectrum you fall on. Plus, you've already taken the quiz from earlier in the book. That's the first step—self-awareness. In some ways, that's the easy part. Once you've figured that out, the next step is to communicate how you operate in a kind, patient way to the people closest to you. Your spouse/partner in life and any business partners you have will benefit from understanding clearly how you best process information and critically think. It's similar to them understanding how your energy works. It will just make everything easier.

Fifty

No Excuses or Limitations

This is the tough love chapter. Fair warning! If you're not a fan of tough love or if you're not in the right headspace for it right now, feel free to skip to the next chapter. I say tough love because it really is love. I care about each and every person who picks up this book. We are kindred spirits, even if we may never meet. (Sidenote: If you ever see me at a conference or in an airport, please do stop and say hello. It truly makes my day when that happens.)

Okay, time for the tough love. Yes, being an introvert is a superpower in many ways, yet there are still some agents who use it as an excuse to not put in the work or do the hard things. You are better than that. The purpose of deeply understanding one's own personality and temperament is not to use it as an excuse; it is to make strategic choices about how you spend your time and energy.

An example of what not to do: Tell yourself you are an introvert so you can't (or won't) talk to people and try to find clients to help. Instead, say, "I'm an introvert, so I'm going to choose lead generation tactics that I enjoy and can commit to doing consistently." We do have to talk to people. We have to talk to a lot of people. That's the nature of being in real estate, and there's really no avoiding it. Embrace it and find ways to make it work for you. Hopefully, you've learned some helpful strategies by reading this book.

Talk to people, then take a nap. Talk to more people, then read some fiction or watch TV. Then go to bed and do it all over again the next day and the next day until your day off. This is our reality. I hope you find it exciting and worth it. If not, perhaps being a real estate agent is not the most aligned role for you. And if that's the case, that's okay! There are plenty of other roles you can have within the real estate industry that involve less sales and less "peopleing." You could be an appraiser, work on a real estate team as a marketing or operations manager, or join forces with a staging company to prepare vacant listings for sale, to name a few options. There is no failure in shifting gears and choosing a different path. I've reinvented myself many times. If anything, it makes you stronger. Your quality of life almost always improves, as well.

If continuing as a real estate agent is your true calling and your desired path, that's fantastic, too. Use what you've learned in this book and through the Quiet Success Club mastermind calls to grow your business the best way possible. Use your strengths. You've got this.

While there are many, many success stories out there, I'd like to share one in particular with you. Ann Cummings is an agent in Portsmouth, New Hampshire who shared her story about dealing with shyness. I hope it will resonate and encourage you to build your business and become a leader in the real estate industry, if that's the path you desire:

> "I think I knew from fairly early on that I was definitely not an outgoing person. I would struggle to join in on conversations. I wasn't and still am not comfortable just walking up to people and joining in on conversations unless I know them really well. I have been extremely shy my whole life, and I still am a very quiet, reserved, shy person.
>
> When I got into real estate as an agent, everyone told me that I was too quiet and shy to succeed and become a real estate agent. The only person who felt I'd do well was my dad. He was also a very shy and quiet person, despite being a pilot in the Air Force. I had to work extra hard to make myself talk to people I didn't know, ask clients questions to help them find the right house, and deal with issues that came up. Over time, I could deal with the shyness although it still overwhelms me in various situations. I have been a real estate agent since 1981, and over those years, I took on several positions within the real estate industry, including local board President, and later on I became State President for New Hampshire Association of REALTORS. I was also active at the National Association of REALTORS, serving on the Board of Directors and vari-

ous committees. Each of those took extra energy and effort on my part to overcome in various degrees my shyness, which I still struggle with. My mom always told me that my shyness made me a much better listener than most people. To this day, I still struggle with shyness, having to force myself at times to take part in conversations."

Ann Cummings

Fifty-One
Thriving in Real Estate Operations

This section was generously written by Hallie Warner, co-author of the best-selling books *The Founder & The Force Multiplier* **and** *The 200% Life*

I've always loved real estate. I took the real estate licensing class in college and started interviewing with real estate firms before graduation. When I was twenty-five, I landed a role as a Listing Assistant for a very successful real estate team. Perfect, I thought. This will be the optimal training ground to learn the ins and outs of the real estate business before I take the leap to commission-only agent and star in my own Bravo series, *Selling Vermont*.

Three months into the role, this introvert knew that heading down the path of Realtor extraordinaire was not for me. But what I had discovered was that my natural introversion—my desire for solitude, deep work and thinking, my insatiable curiosity and desire to learn, and my ability to sit in one place and crank through projects for a long period of time—was best suited to the career path I was already on. Behind the scenes. Building the foundation for the business. Supporting our agents and rainmaker and allowing them to live in their strengths. While creating an environment where we could all thrive.

As Susan Cain explains in *Quiet*, introverts have a preference for a minimally stimulating environment. We tend to enjoy quiet concentration, listen more than we talk, think before we speak, and approach risk with caution. Contrary to common misconceptions, we are not anti-social; we are differently social. In real estate operations, these qualities can be a distinct advantage.

If you're an introvert who loves real estate but dreads the idea of being in sales, don't worry—there's a perfect place for you in the industry.

Operations specialists (which include titles such as Director of Operations, Executive Assistant, Client Care Manager, or COO) play a crucial role in supporting agents and building successful businesses behind the scenes and beside their leader.

The Quiet Power of Introverts in Real Estate Operations

Introverts as operations specialists bring a wealth of valuable skills to the real estate industry. Operations specialists use their strengths in organization, strategy, and deep work to create the foundation that keeps a real estate team running efficiently and growing strategically.

Here are some of the most powerful strengths you can leverage as an introvert:

- **Quiet Confidence**: Confidence doesn't mean you have all the answers or know everything. Confidence is being secure in knowing that you can find a solution to any challenge that comes your way. Operations specialists don't have to be the loudest voice in the room to be effective. You lead through influence and by example.

- **Deep Listening**: You excel at listening, absorbing information, and asking powerful questions that help people think differently and influence decisions. You thoughtfully contribute for the good of the team.

- **Strategic Thinking & Analysis**: Your ability to reflect, analyze, and think critically means you can anticipate problems before they arise and create efficient systems to keep the business running smoothly. You have a natural ability to triangulate information, understand underlying problems, and offer creative solutions to challenges before anyone even realizes they need them.

- **Careful Observation**: You notice the little things that others might miss, which makes you invaluable in keeping track of details, improving workflows, and creating high-impact experiences for your team, customers, and clients.

Best Practices for Working with Extroverted Team Members

Working with a loud, extroverted leader or agent can be a challenge for an introverted real estate assistant, but it can also be a powerful partnership. Here are some best practices for communicating effectively while also managing your energy:

1. **Leverage Written Communication**: Extroverts thrive on fast verbal communication, but you may need time to process. Written communication will help you organize your thoughts and ensure clarity. Consider creating asynchronous communication systems, such as project management software, voice notes, or weekly briefings to allow you to collect your thoughts and respond thoughtfully.

2. **Schedule Structured Check-Ins**: Instead of ad-hoc conversations, set regular one-on-one meetings with your rainmaker or other team members, as needed, to discuss priorities, updates, and challenges. This allows for focused, productive discussions without constant interruptions. And because large meetings can be overwhelming, these one-on-one discussions can be a great way to share your insights and contribute without the pressure of a crowd.

3. **Use Your Strength of Deep Listening**: Extroverts thrive on bouncing ideas off others. By listening carefully and asking clarifying questions, you can extract key information, connect the dots among seemingly disparate ideas, catch problems before they arise, highlight winning ideas, and fol-

low up with thoughtful suggestions and solutions. This can help your rainmaker and team stay on track and save time by only acting on the best ideas.

4. **Create a System for Prioritization**: Extroverted leaders often throw multiple ideas around at once. And they are all important and need to be completed immediately. Or so they would have you think. But you can help them slow down (just a little). Implement a system to track, prioritize, and filter what truly needs action, so you don't get swept up in the chaos. Refer back to this system during your one-on-one meetings to ensure alignment and that you are all making progress on the right projects.

5. **Set Clear Expectations for Response Time**: Extroverts' energy can sometimes be overwhelming, but remember that their enthusiasm isn't a demand for an immediate response. However, it is important to have a conversation about what is expected as it relates to response time, communication methods, and more. Let your rainmaker know that you may need time to process or do additional research before responding, and find a communication style that works for both of you.

Thriving in an Extroverted Industry

The real estate industry offers so many opportunities. And there is a special spot in real estate operations for introverts. Your ability to create order, provide strategic analysis, and lead with quiet confidence is what allows salespeople to do what they do best.

Remember, while you may operate behind the scenes, that doesn't mean your voice needs to take a back seat. Quiet leadership is powerful.

Fifty-Two

Morning Routine and Evening Wind Down

Most of us have a morning and evening routine, even if we don't realize it. We brush our teeth, change clothes, and shower in the mornings and/or evenings. Maybe we eat. Maybe we stretch or exercise. This is not the book in which you learn how to create the perfect morning or evening routine based on what someone else does (*The Miracle Morning for Real Estate Agents* by Hal Elrod and Michael J. Maher is a fantastic book if you want to see what others do). This is where you learn how to curate your own habits to make them work best for you as an individual.

Start with an audit of what you currently do. Write it down. What are your normal habits most mornings and evenings? It will vary somewhat, but I'm sure you can pinpoint the activities you do consistently and the order in which you typically do them. We are not talking about what you'd like to do; be completely honest with yourself during this audit. Whether you run ten miles every morning or eat ice cream every single night, don't judge it. Just write it down.

Then assess how each aspect affects you. How does it make you feel? How does it affect your productivity? Your mindset? Your health? Your sleep? Your relationship with your family/partner? This is a lot, and it can be time-consuming to ask these questions of each and every aspect of both your morning and evening routines. It will be worth it. This is the only way to truly understand your choices and their impact on you.

After you've assessed your routines, decide what to do. Maybe you are already making the best choices and there's nothing left to improve. That's unlikely, but there could be one or two people out there who have perfected their routines, and that would be excellent. More than likely, there will be things you can improve: do more of, do less of, remove entirely, or add in. Create your new plan for both morning and night.

Keep in mind your goals for both the morning and the evening. For most of us, the evening goal is to improve sleep quality. For some of us, the morning goal is to be as energized and productive as possible. However, allow for variations on these goals. Create your own goals, and know they can change. During an exceptionally stressful period in my career, my morning goal shifted from productivity to calm. I started reading fiction for a half hour first thing in the morning. I wouldn't let myself think about the work I had to do until I got to the office. During that season of life, that's what I needed, and I allowed myself to adjust my routine accordingly.

MOVE OVER EXTROVERTS

One last piece of advice: Start with changing one thing at a time. Don't change up your entire routine at once—it's too much. Take your time. Feel it out, and tweak as needed. Remember doing science experiments in school and testing different variables? It was key to only change one variable at a time to accurately gauge its effect. The same is true here. One change at a time also increases the likelihood you'll stick with it. Building new habits isn't easy, but it's worth the effort.

Fifty-Three
The Fake Smile

Another incredible tool in an introvert's toolbox is the fake smile. I know I told you not to be inauthentic, but the fake smile is a loophole. Sometimes it's necessary. Sometimes smiling and agreeing requires less energy than getting into a long, deep conversation with someone you can't stand about something you don't care about. I'm sure you've been in that situation before. The fake smile is polite while allowing you to exit a conversation with grace.

Every conversation you have is an output of energy. You must use this energy wisely. Remember, energy is a finite resource and a tool in your toolbox. There's only so much of it at any given moment, and it's up to you how you spend it. Imagine you had to pay one hundred dollars for every conversation you have. It's the same concept—draining of resources. So using a fake smile on occasion is an unfortunate necessity. It will allow you to use your energy with people who inspire a genuine smile.

Fifty-Four

Find Peace and Become a Better Agent

I'm so thankful you've chosen to read this book and hope you'll implement some of what you have learned to create a better life for yourself. True understanding of self leads to better choices in your business and your life. Better allocation of resources: time, energy, and money. It also leads to more peace, less stress. You will become calm. Intentional. You will have more ownership over your decisions and the results they produce. That's empowering, not scary. Own it. Your confidence will grow. You will attract your ideal clients.

The best real estate agents are the most self-aware, disciplined, and hyper-focused on the activities that have the biggest impact and are most aligned with who they are. This will be you if it's not already. I have faith in you. You can do this. Take breaks. Take care of yourself first. And enjoy this life as a powerful, intelligent, calm, peaceful introvert.

Take Action:

- Take a deep breath and journal. Process everything you just learned.

- If you haven't already, share with the people closest to you that you are an introvert; share your specific energy-recharging needs with them so they understand.

- Create your morning and evening routines. Make small tweaks to whatever you are currently doing. Do not try to change everything at once.

- Join your fellow introverted agents in our Facebook community: "Introverts in Real Estate."

- Access all the downloads and extras mentioned throughout the book at: www.MoveOverExtroverts.com/Bonus

Acknowledgements

Thank you to the individuals who generously contributed their words and their wisdom to this book: Chelsea Anderson, Ann Cummings, Michael Heissenbuttel, Janine Sasso, Heather Schmidt, Erica Smentowski, Ryan Smith, and Hallie Warner.

Thank you, Matthew Pollard, for your incredibly valuable advice and insights about the book-writing and book-selling processes. It's an honor to call you a mentor.

Thank you to everyone who has been with me on this journey, encouraged me, hired me to teach classes, to speak at conferences, and to coach. Thank you to everyone who participates in our Facebook community, and to all the members of the Quiet Success Club.

Thank you to my parents for their love and support.

And thank you to Keith, for being my biggest cheerleader, my partner in all things, and my favorite extrovert.

References

Buelow, Beth. 2015. *The Introvert Entrepreneur: Amplify Your Strengths and Create Success on Your Own Terms.* Tarcher Perigee.

Cain, Susan. 2013. *Quiet: The Power of Introverts in the World That Can't Stop Talking.* Crown.

"Empire Building Podcast." Keller Williams. Video, https://go.kw.com/empire-building.

"Irish Goodbye." Neologisms. Rice, Accessed February 8, 2025.

Mackler, Carolyn. 2024. *The Wife App.* Simon & Schuster.

Maher , Michael J. 2010. *The 7 Levels of Communication.* Author House Bloomington.

"Mental Load: What It Is and how to Manage It." UCLA Health, January 8, 2024. https://www.uclahealth.org/news/article/mental-load-what-it-and-how-manage-it.

Olson, Eric J. "How Many Hours of Sleep Are Enough for Good Health?" Mayo Clinic. February 1, 2025. https://www.mayoclinic.org/healthy-lifestyle/adult-health/expert-answers/how-many-hours-of-sleep-are-enough/faq-20057898.

Papasan, Jay, and Keller, Gary. 2012. *The ONE Thing: The Surprisingly Simple Truth About Extraordinary Results*. Bard Press.

Pilat D., & Sekoul D. (2021). In-group Bias. The Decision Lab. Retrieved February 7, 2025.

Pollard, Matthew. 2018. *The Introvert's Edge*. Amacom.

"The Science of Asking for What We Want in Business and in Life." BNI New Zealand. March 2, 2023. Accessed February 8, 2025.

Sinek, Simon. 2009. *Start with Why: How Great Leaders Inspire Everyone to Take Action*. Portfolio.

Smith, Ryan. Local Expert Academy. Accessed February 8, 2025.

Solon, Matthew. "How Much Sleep Do You Actually Need?" Harvard Health Publishing. October 30,

2023. https://www.health.harvard.edu/blog/how-much-sleep-do-you-actually-need-202310302986.

"Success with Real Estate Mailers, Success with Just Listed & Just Sold Postcards, or Success with Sphere & Past Client Postcards." The Hyperlocal Agent. Accessed February 8, 2025.

Recommended Reading

- *The Introvert Entrepreneur* - Beth Buelow

- *Quiet* - Susan Cain

- *The Miracle Morning for Real Estate Agents* - Hal Elrod & Michael J Maher

- *Exactly What to Say for Real Estate Agents* - Phil Jones, Chris Smith, Jimmy Mackin

- *The Millionaire Real Estate Agent* - Gary Keller, Jay Papasan, Dave Jenks

- *The Art of War for Real Estate Agents* - Keith Krikorian

- *The 7 Levels of Communication* - Michael J Maher

- *The One Thing* - Gary Keller and Jay Papasan

- *The Introvert's Edge* - Matthew Pollard

- *Success With Real Estate Mailers* - Janine Sasso

- *Fierce Conversation* - Susan Scott

- *Start With Why* - Simon Sinek

- *The Full Fee Agent* - Chris Voss & Steve Shull

- *Never Split the Difference* - Chris Voss

- *The Mountain Is You* - Brianna Wiest

www.ingramcontent.com/pod-product-compliance
Lightning Source LLC
Jackson TN
JSHW020903130425
82508JS00001B/2